mentor in Maine.
I couldn't help
thinking you'd like
it.   — Mindy

Strenuous Blessings

Strenuous Blessings

a book of essays

Mary Cushman

Bennetts Cove Books
Casco Bay, Maine

ISBN-13: 978-0-692-93451-7

Cover Photo: James M. Thresher
An amended version of "The Widow's Mite" was published in Down East Magazine in March 2017

for Tom

We are put on earth a little while to learn to bear the beams of love.

William Blake

Every love is carved from loss. Mine was. Yours is. Your great-great-great grandchildren's will be. But we learn to live in that love.

Jonathan Safran Foer

Contents

Preface

All strenuous blessings are ambiguous and require a capacity to see the challenges of our lives in *both/and* terms. Think of a remark that bites . . . and that you know is laced with deep truth. Or consider a spouse aggravatingly quick to flare up in anger...and just as quick to seek forgiveness. Or contemplate a much-loved, aging mother you've invited to come live with you...and soon she's mistaking windows for doors, asking you, her middle-aged daughter, "Where do I know you from?"

Such "blessings" may feel more like curses because the ambiguity in them can tax us severely. And yet when the casing around these blessings is cracked like a shell and falls away, a strong glint of gold will likely get revealed. Strenuous blessings are difficult *and* full of grace. And once integrated into our spiritual bloodstream, they fuel the growth of gratitude in us—gratitude for the rough as well as the smooth.

If one of the chief tasks of a spiritual life is the development of a grateful heart, the road to such a heart will include many strenuous blessings. And yet, while these may be easily discerned, embracing them is not so easy. A casual, unambiguous blessing can be received as lightly as a summer breeze. But blessings that require us to stay open to painful experiences and emotions and then live fully into a complex gratitude—those are hard.

The essays in this book are about the significance of certain blessed and ambiguous experiences on the formation of my own grateful heart. One essay, for instance, explores the emotional pitfalls of being a stepmother without having had my own children. Another looks at the unexpected resonance of a relationship with a person unable to speak.

Embracing the strenuous blessings in our lives means allowing ourselves to be pruned by forces more powerful than our own limited egos and desires. It means living into whatever hand life deals us—with as much courage as we can muster. I don't mean we're supposed to endure all sorts of life situations that are damaging to us. But *any* hand we are dealt is likely to include its share of hardships, each of which will affect whether gratitude or some form of ingratitude settles inside us.

For me, the road to a grateful heart has been strewn with potholes, peopled by shadowy figures, frequently edged with distress. I've encountered many dark emotions along the way, ever eager to take up residence in me—wily adversaries like envy, defensiveness, self-pity. And even when these adversaries are mostly vanquished, even when heartache and gratitude finally sing together, a descant of sadness can remain.

At least it remains in me. "We are put on earth a little while to learn to bear the beams of love," said William Blake. Those beams of love are usually heavy *and* light, joyful *and* sad. And they can be nailed together with demanding ironies. Learning to bear them to the shores of gratitude is a lifelong spiritual journey—one on which it's not always possible to walk with head held high.

To live into the strenuous blessings of our lives means emigrating from the narrow landscape of *either/or*, and bravely pressing on into the far more demanding but rewarding country of *both/and*. In practical terms, how do we do this? We invite the biting remark to penetrate us—and commit ourselves to pursuing the truth in it. We don't allow our partner with the fiery temper to oppress us with it—and we rejoice in the balm that eventually comes from conflict resolved, forgiveness freely given. We steer a mother, without scolding, away from the window toward the door and seek the strength to endure the pain of no longer being known by her. It's all a matter of *both/and*. And to be fair we can't always do this. It is sometimes extremely difficult to live fully into the hand we are dealt. But by yielding, eventually, where we can, to the deep ambiguity in the strenuous blessings that do come our way, the sweet, ripe fruit of gratitude will finally drop and spill its seed.

In an important sense, the full meaning of these blessings usually becomes clear only after we have looked long in a rearview mirror. We need plenty of time to reflect, to weigh, to ask *what if*, and *what if not*, and to get our arms opened wide enough. When we are granted the time and the grace to do that reflecting, to get our arms sufficiently outstretched, gratitude can then order our hearts and our days.

You Rich

I walked to school in the morning; by afternoon, I couldn't walk.

A week later our doctor, an intimate friend of my family and someone my thirteen-year-old self had God-like faith in, sat down on my bed at home and said, with relief, "Well, at least you don't have polio." In 1955, those words were welcome indeed.

"What do I have then, Sam?"

"We don't know yet. I think you may have rheumatic fever, but I want to send you to the hospital for tests to figure it out."

My mother stood in a corner of the room, her arms crossed and her mouth set—whether from fear, or aggravation, or both, I couldn't tell. I had two younger sisters, the hospital was a half hour's distance, she was a busy woman. I turned my face away from her, toward Sam.

"Will I get better?" I asked him, my anxiety rising.

"Of course, you will," he said, patting my arm.

The ambulance driver switched on his siren and we wailed out of the parking lot, my parents following in our family station wagon. I'd been at the diagnostic hospital for ten days. I was now being transferred, with more fanfare than seemed required, to a nearby rehabilitation hospital for children with rheumatic fever and related illnesses. Tucked onto a mattress behind the driver's seat, I looked up through the ambulance windows at the overcast sky and watched treetops toss in the early March wind. Everything I loved—parents, sisters, cats, dog, friends, family suppers, all that spelled home—was receding backward at a disorienting tilt, while successive telephone poles marked the ambulance's forward progress, to the beat of my fearful heart.

Three times a day in the rehab hospital, kids congregated to receive medications at a dispensing window in the hall outside my room. Normally, the window was shuttered with a grimy aluminum grate and the hall was silent. But during meds the area was bedlam: loud shouts, wild shoving, Technicolor swearing, unending laughter. Many kids jigged restlessly up and down, afflicted with the jerky rhythms of St. Vitus's dance; other kids got angry being jostled out of line by the jerking. A proctor insisting on quiet usually surrendered in defeat.

This daily ruckus mattered to me greatly because, during my brief tenure in that room, pain shadowed every breath I took and noise aggravated it like chalk on a blackboard from hell. I'd been told that eventually the excruciating joint pain I had would subside. For now, though, it occupied every intersection of my body, and excessive noise caused my tender girlish self to want to take a hatchet to the nearest neck. The pain was particularly acute in my wrists. The nurse's aide who once—only once—flung back the sheets under my resting wrists lived permanently in the Seventh Circle.

That room was my introduction to Irvington House. Perched high above the Hudson River, slightly north of New York City, in a seedy old Gothic mansion, the place was a first-rate medical facility—according to Sam. He had an additional reason to want me there: it was close enough to our town, a bit farther north in Westchester County, along the Hudson, so that he was able to come visit me.

My first indication about where I'd landed, and what I might expect, came from a girl named Lorraine who appeared in my room during one of the medication melees. She was sixteen and had been a resident at Irvington House for about three years—going home periodically to her family in the Bronx, and always returning. When she saw I was in pain, she quickly made her purpose clear.

"You need to understand something," she said, in a strong New York accent. "There are four white girls here, and you and I are two of them. The rest of the kids are Negro, or Spanish, or a mix. Some of them may not be too nice to you. Especially at first. I'm not saying anyone will hurt you, they just may not always be nice. I'll help you when I can." She flashed me a reassuring smile through the freckles strewn across her pale, Irish face and slipped back out the door.

I soon got a dose of Lorraine's warning. Once the medications took hold and my joints calmed down, I was moved onto a ward with a dozen other girls, ages roughly eight to fifteen, all of them light cocoa colored to dark chocolate. None of them was unfriendly, exactly, but they kept their distance.

During the daytime, we attended a facsimile of school, in the building's basement, about eighty boys and girls total. Tossed together into a few classrooms, no one fussed over the grade levels we actually belonged in; the chief hope was to keep us corralled, occupied, and tempered to a dull roar. Some of us, like me, were confined to wheelchairs all day, in school and out. Bed rest was a requirement for early stage rheumatic fever and being allowed into a wheelchair was considered activity enough. At that, someone else had to wheel us everywhere.

Kids who had graduated from wheelchairs to the ambulatory wards of the hospital were allowed to roam the halls and play outside when we weren't in school. In its heyday, the one-time mansion had been surrounded by expansive, manicured lawns; these had long since been replaced by blacktopped parking lots, playing fields, and a baseball diamond.

Participation in outdoor activities conferred a coveted status—it meant one was in the pipeline for discharge. The rest of us were reminded of our lesser estate by a constant stream of sing-song taunts and insults, heaped on us while others played: bedridden baby, no-legs-girl, sick-ass fatso, never walk again pussy-face or dickhead, depending on your equipment. Nurses, doctors and other staff tried to stem the tide of these jeers. But they were mostly hurled beyond authority's earshot. Especially at night.

My second night on the ward, I was doing what I'd done every night since I arrived at Irvington House—crying hot tears into my pillow. I was wrenched inside out with homesickness and felt as though my heart would break from the weight of it. Eventually, of course, I cried myself to sleep and woke the next day hearing anew my mother's exhortations to be brave, to buck up. Those words were barely effective in the daytime; at night, they dissolved into fresh tears.

I tried to stifle the crying, fearful of the ridicule it could bring. It wasn't a complete surprise, therefore, but it scared me plenty, when four or five figures materialized around my bed, their dark faces invisible, and began whispering, both boys and girls, "Crybaby, crybaby, little white girl want her mother's milk?" They then threw multiple glasses of water at me and fled under a blanket of muffled laughter. Drenched, I reared up and yelled. To little avail. By the time the night nurse registered the commotion and waddled onto the ward with a flashlight, the boys had melted into the walls, the girls had slid back into beds somewhere nearby. I didn't have any idea who'd done it.

And if I'd known I wouldn't have told, sure that tattling would only make things worse. Even when Sam came to see me the next day, a visit that was balm to my spirit, I kept quiet—not wanting him to throw his doctor's weight around on my behalf. A similar scene got repeated for another couple of nights, again soaking me, the bedclothes, and the floor under the bed. The nurse on night duty rotated, so each night it was somebody new muttering through the mopping up. No one got caught or punished.

In the midst of this siege, a Sunday rolled around—the only day visitors were allowed. My parents came for the first time, and at last I was enveloped in the hugs I'd yearned for. When I showed them a painting I'd done for them in school, now ruined by the nighttime deluges, they were outraged on my behalf. I convinced them it was just teenaged mischief. With Lorraine's inside track, I now knew who the players were and I definitely didn't want to rat on those particular kids. Besides, I was so happy to see my parents and to banish the homesickness even for a little while that I eagerly minimized the trouble. Unfortunately, their visit ushered in more of it.

First of all, I realized with a start that they looked like wealthy people. I'd always been keenly aware they weren't, but now my mother's camel's hair coat and pearl earrings and my father's tweed jacket and bow tie said otherwise. Loudly. At the least, they looked very different from the few other parents coming on and off the ward— none of whom were wearing tweed.

Secondly, they brought me something that inadvertently breathed money. Sitting on the bed, full of bustle and excitement, my mother prompted my father to pull a little box out of his pocket while she exclaimed that they'd had a special present made for me. It was a delicate gold ring, with intricate curlicues and a sapphire, my birth-stone, in the center, offset by tiny diamond chips. It was my first grown-up present. My mother made it plain that the ring had cost plenty and I understood, partly because it *was* an extravagance, that it was meant to be treasured for a lifetime. When she slipped it onto my finger, however, clucking with satisfaction, and I crooned in grateful delight, my spirits steadily sank. I was certain that when the other kids saw this ring I'd be branded: rich beyond imagining.

Which is exactly what happened. That night, as I reckoned with the heaviness I felt in the wake of my parents' departure and the piercing realization that they wouldn't be back for a very long week, my tears and my tormentors arrived together. But that night there was more than tossed water.

"Give that ring," someone commanded, as they crowded around my bed. I recognized the voice of Judy, the big, tough girl in the bed two down from mine. She'd had no visitors that day. "We seen it," she whispered. "We seen your fancy-ass parents give it and we want it." They grabbed my hand, trying to wrench the ring off my finger. Two other kids pinned me to the bed. They hadn't thought to cover my mouth, though, and this time I screamed bloody murder.

"The water, the water," one of the boys blurted out. "Drown her!" And they tried to, but they had to bolt off the ward or into nearby beds because I kept on screaming. We all knew the night nurse would show up fast at this sustained howl and she did come running—profoundly aggravated. Sizing up the scene, she moved me into the room I'd been in when I first arrived. It had once been a hated location, but was now a haven next to her and her all-night light. In the morning, she asked to have me transferred to a ward just for children on bed rest, with a nurse always on duty. Feeling as though I'd been delivered from Purgatory, I was to remain on this ward for the rest of my time at Irvington House—not exempt from further trouble, but with a certain sense of being cordoned off.

Before my parents showed up the next Sunday to visit, I had decided to give the ring back to them for safe-keeping. I'd endured too much derision for it, with more threats to steal it. Lorraine was a big help in this, convincing me that few of the kids would ever be friendly as long as I looked like the rich girl on the block.

My parents were unhappy with my return of the ring to them. When I revealed just enough of what I'd been experiencing, though, they acquiesced and were relieved to find me on a new ward.

"I know Sam would approve of your being moved," my mother said. I told her I wasn't sure Sam knew much about this hospital when he recommended it. She sniffed.

"I think you need to leave that up to his judgment. He feels strongly that you will get the best care here and you're not in a position to question him about that."

She was right on the medical caring score—mostly. I relayed to my parents that I was forever being monitored: blood draws every other day, weekly echocardiograms, a non-stop diet of cortisone and penicillin. And bed rest until I thought it would drive me crazy.

"Those are the rules, kid," my father said, with a sweet smile, knowing I wouldn't be disobedient. What neither of them knew because I didn't tell them, was my very disobedient response to a doctor I had seen earlier that week. In a small, private office he had his stethoscope on my chest and stood uncomfortably close to me. With my hospital Johnny dropped down around my waist, he began to rub my emerging breasts and said, with a smile-that-wasn't-a-smile, "Where'd you get these?" I barely understood what he was doing, but understood enough to push his hand away. He scowled, stopped, and quickly dispatched me to my wheelchair and an aide.

Although the incident continued to unnerve me, talking to Lorraine quieted my anxiety. It had happened to other girls, she said. But she also told me this doctor seldom visited Irvington House patients and that I probably wouldn't have to see him again. Especially since I'd pushed him away. That kind of steadying presence from Lorraine had begun to fill in the cracks created by my parents' absence. When they left after this second visiting day, I realized I'd started to make my own way. I still missed them terribly, and yet I saw that they couldn't take care of me here. I had to manage without them.

On one of the ambulatory wards there was a Spanish boy named Julio. He was fifteen, tall for his age, and over-weight. He'd broken his leg in a recent outdoor skirmish and now walked with a large cast. A cast that knocked on the hallway floors, hard and loud, with every advancing step.

Julio had started following me around. My white skin didn't deter *him*; in school, he found reasons to sit next to me. On the playing fields, he hung around my wheelchair like a bird with a broken wing. A very large bird. I didn't like him. I told him—not politely—to leave me alone. But he was impervious to my newfound swearwords. They just inflamed his interest.

One day Lorraine approached me with a look of con-cern—not her usual face.

"You need to watch out for Julio," she said. When I asked why, she replied, "He's been boasting about 'mak-ing you his girlfriend.' Which means, around this place, figuring out a way to get in your pants. By force, if neces-sary." I felt a cold sword run through my belly.

"What am I supposed to do?"

"For one thing, let me wheel you everywhere in your chair—including the bathroom. Don't let anyone else take you places. When Julio and his friends see me doing that, they'll think twice." I knew this was probably true. Lorraine had had a few dust-ups of her own here. Despite being white, she was respected by the kids for being both tough and fair-minded. And the staff trusted her, which all the kids knew.

"Also," she went on, "tell Mrs. Jackson. As the nurse on your ward, she needs to know about this and to clue in the night nurse."

"But Julio wouldn't come on my ward, would he?"

She gave me a look to squelch my naiveté. "He might decide that you're craving one of his special kisses and he just has to deliver it."

For the next few days, with Lorraine glued to my wheelchair, Julio receded into the background. I still caught an occasional smirk, and one time he leered at me and licked his lips, but he stopped latching onto me.

What didn't stop, though, was the knocking of his cast in the hall outside the ward. I could hear him, alone or with other kids, going by a few times each day and night. The sound unnerved me, but by now it was too much a part of the hospital landscape for me to call any nursing attention to it. Besides, he never paused at the ward door or came inside. Until he did.

It was after lunch. Mrs. Jackson was elsewhere; most of the other kids on the ward had been wheeled off to medical appointments. I was in my bed, turned away from the door, absorbed in a book. I was only dimly aware of the silence that always followed the stopped knocking of the cast. In a flash, Julio flung himself over my bed, all his weight on top of me, and yanked my hair to pull my head around.

"You're going to kiss me," he growled, "if it's the last thing you ever do." I pressed my lips together as tightly as I could, but he forced his big tongue into my mouth, breathing hard, grinding my face. Suddenly he stopped. Mrs. Jackson, all ninety pounds of her furious coal-black self leaning hard into the task, had hauled him off me.

"Any more behavior like this, Julio de Jesus," she hissed, "and you will be on your way back to New York City. I mean it. And I understand you have worse in mind for her. Hear me, boy: if you lay another hand on her, for any reason, you are done. Out. Finished. And they won't let you come back because I'll make sure they don't. Now get off this ward. And don't ever show your face here again."

After establishing that a fumbling French kiss was the whole of it, Mrs. Jackson gave my hair a tender stroke, shook her head, and returned to her tasks. Miranda, the Negro girl in the bed next to mine who had been taking all this in, rolled her eyes at me. She offered a shy smile and asked if I wanted to play cards. I could have cried with relief—for a dozen reasons. As April sunshine streamed through the ward's dirty windows, warming everything it fell on, Miranda dealt the cards.

A couple of days later, Sam visited me and I was able to greet him more happily than the last time. He was encouraged—if puzzled.

"I don't get it," he said. "It's not at all clear you have rheumatic fever. You've had many of the symptoms, and we're going to keep treating you as though you have it, but so far your heart seems fine, so there's a lot less to worry about than I once thought." Having no understanding of the potential horrors of this disease, I eagerly embraced his optimism.

"Can I go home soon?"

"Not for quite a while, honey. We have to be really sure what's going on with you, so I'm afraid you're here for some time to come. Maybe as long as another couple of months. Can you stand it?"

"This is a hard place, Sam. It's a rough place. I mean, the hospital people are mostly good, but a lot of the kids are rough."

He gave my shoulder a firm, affectionate squeeze. "Just do your best," he said. "Do everything the doctors and nurses tell you and try not to get too discouraged about the kids. Many of them come from difficult family situations, a lot of poverty. Think about that when you find them rough. You'll get out of here and have the privilege of spending the rest of the summer on your island in Maine. None of them will do that. They'll go back to New York City, most of them, to a far different life from yours. And because they often can't get the care they need, many will just cycle through here again."

"Will I have to come back?"

"Very unlikely. That's why I want you to stay until it's truly time for you to go. Don't worry. I talk to your doctors all the time. I promise you won't be here a day more than necessary."

Long after Sam left, this conversation continued to echo through me. I'd never really thought about what privilege might mean, never thought of my own life as "privileged." I'd taken my life for granted, even when this illness struck me out of the blue. It hadn't occurred to me that everything might not come around right, in the end, for all of us hospitalized here. Indeed: it had never occurred to me before that my perspective—or my fortunes—differed from others. By age thirteen I knew it was harder to be dark-skinned than light-skinned, but I knew it only because my parents had told me. I had no firsthand experience of discrimination, except what I had now learned the hard way at the hands of other kids at this hospital. My anguish over that treatment was real. And yet the anguish itself also gave me an early, indispensable glimmer of insight into just how radically my skin color would spare me.

After the incident with Julio the ground shifted. Miranda wasn't the only friendly one; some of the other girls couldn't wait to talk to me. For a couple of days, I swam in a sea of black and tan faces, egging me on to retell the story, all of them relishing the image of Julio nailed in midflight. It seemed I wasn't his only victim—one girl got badly bruised by his advances and was a minor celebrity for kicking him where it counted.

Some of the boys, too, were nicer to me. One even told me he was sorry he had thrown water on me. I continued to feel harassed sometimes and the name-calling, when it happened, still stung. But there were a few defenders now—sometimes even protectors. Julio's offensive had given me a little status, a certain currency in the bank. And while Lorraine remained my chief companion and ally, the hedge against loneliness was thickening with new blooms.

Despite these social gains, the medical picture remained inconclusive. As a consequence, I was frustrated by orders to stay in bed. Spring had descended on the Hudson River Valley, and I was wild to join others in the games I could hear on the grounds below my windows. Instead, I had to settle for my brief forays onto our third floor, stone balcony, waving down and yearning, locked up as tight as Rapunzel.

In a collateral piece of medical fallout, I'd gained a lot of weight, like many other kids there. Stuffed full of cortisone, and fed well, most of us sported large, round, full moon faces. My mother was particularly agitated by this. In some subtle way, she seemed to blame me for being overweight, which only increased my conviction of always being at fault in her eyes.

Her alarm about my increasing size reached galactic levels when we arrived at the day in late May for the Irvington House School Graduation Ceremony. I was graduating from eighth grade and a dress she brought from home didn't fit. Not by a long shot. The day was humid and hot—she was bad tempered. I was a fat, sweaty, moon-faced failure. I was also distraught about the news that I'd have to graduate from a wheelchair. We had an epic argument; I graduated in the wheelchair, decked out in an old pair of pajamas. Nobody noticed or cared about the pajamas except my mother, who departed that afternoon with both of us in an unresolved frenzy of hurt feelings.

When May gave way to June, two things happened. First, my father came to tell me I would probably be released from Irvington House within a month. It was hard to believe; I could almost smell the salty winds of summer blowing from Maine and taste the wild strawberries that I knew were ripening.

"No getting out of bed, though, kid," he said. "Not until they give the word."

"But *nobody* leaves here from bed, Daddy, ever. Everybody has to be up and walking first."

"Not you," he said, trying to look stern. "Promise me. In bed." Despite the ponies galloping through my veins, I promised him.

Secondly, I'd begun to make friends for real, and this laid a stripe of ambivalence down through my feelings like white paint on a highway. I didn't want to stay at Irvington House, I wanted to go home. But I also wanted to hold onto these friends, and I realized that when I went, so would the friendships.

Take Miranda, in the bed next to me. We were well beyond cards, especially after Lights Out. One Sunday night when Miranda, yet again, hadn't had any visitors, I asked her why not. She was quiet in the dark. I waited; she sighed.

"My daddy's gone," she said. "And I don't know where my mama is. And my grandma's got no money for the train here." She loved her grandmother very much and I knew that she would be living with her when she left. She spoke to me, though, in chords of loneliness and sadness I hadn't heard before. From her or from anyone else, ever. I reached for her fingers and we fell asleep, holding hands.

And there was Lucia, a five-year-old Spanish girl, thin as a pencil, with corkscrew curls she always wanted me to brush. She was on an ambulatory ward, and visited me often in my unending bed rest. I'd come to adore her and adored her adoption of me.

One Sunday, earlier than my parents were due to show up, Lucia asked if I'd get someone to push my wheelchair to her ward so we could watch together for her mother to arrive. She sat on my lap as we stared out the window at the parking lot three floors down, waiting. She held my wrists tightly with her miniature hands, staying quiet until a tall, stylish, light coffee-colored woman appeared on the pavement below. Lucia squirmed in my arms then, buried her head in my collarbone and said softly, "My mother's a whore." I stiffened. I knew what the word meant but I couldn't imagine it leaping out of this five-year-old rosebud mouth. I hugged her hard, stuck for a response. As her mother disappeared into the building below our sight, Lucia clung to me, her enormous black eyes filled with something I couldn't touch.

And there were other kids, less close, but still important to me. Over the past month a number of them had become more distinct, like bright threads I'd failed to see running through a familiar fabric. Some kids from my initial days there had gone back to New York City, replaced by others I wouldn't stay long enough to know. That was okay. I'd gained my own perch, and was content to occasionally sit in my wheelchair on the edge of the playing fields, in the sun, mostly un-harassed. It was enough to be able to watch softballs get whacked around, to laugh with the others—at nothing and at everything.

On just such a day in late June, I got word that my mother was coming with my sisters in tow. They had all been in Maine to open up our summer cottage, but needed to return home to Westchester for a day and would stop to see me too. Since children weren't usually allowed to visit, I hadn't seen my sisters for almost four months. The prospect was both exhilarating and scary. I looked so weird; my round face, normal in the hospital, now made me shy with embarrassment. I wondered whether they would be agitated at the sight of me, how they'd react to the wheelchair.

Someone wheeled me down to the first floor, where I heard my sisters long before I saw them. At nine and seven, with too much time logged in a car over the past couple of days, I knew they would be ecstatic to be set free. They spotted me down the long hall, ran toward me shouting my name, picked up speed, and then slid to a stop in front of the wheelchair—steamy, flushed, braids askew—breathing hard. They struggled with a plastic container they passed between them, half arguing, more focused on it than on me and my fat face. They finally thrust the container toward me, a small-fry delivery service on a mission.

"*We* picked these!" one said.

"But the plastic got hot in the car so they aren't too great anymore," added the other.

They chewed the ends of their braids and twisted their skinny legs. "Open it, open it," they begged. I thought I'd already guessed the contents from the deep red color I saw through the plastic, but as I screwed off the top I was overcome by the smell of the wild strawberries—masses of them, now heavenly strawberry mush. My sisters knew that every June, soon after we arrived on the island, I would go far afield in search of these tiny morsels of glory. I sank my face into the container and came up for air with a sob stuck in my throat.

"Will you come home soon?" they clamored, as they crowded around the wheelchair, kissing me, trying to get on my lap, wrapping their arms around my neck. I looked up at my mother. She smiled, nodded, and mouthed the words "not long," which brought up both delight and sadness in me—an ambivalent response I could never have imagined when I first came through the doors here.

Barely two weeks later, my father arrived to collect me. I was on the ward getting ready, testing my legs. Not accustomed yet to walking any further than the bathroom,

I needed reassurance from the nurses. But I was quickly returning to my old self—at least outwardly.

In my chest, a sorrowful ache warred with my excitement. I'd spent that morning and a large part of the previous day saying goodbye to nurses, doctors, social workers, and kids. The parting from Lorraine and Lucia struck me, for different reasons, in a quick I hadn't known existed. Miranda had already gone to an ambulatory ward and then been sent home to her grandmother a week ago, which is when the ache had begun for real.

Finally my father appeared—tall and beaming, my life-long source of comfort. He bundled me and my stuff into the wheelchair, "A ride to forget," as he called it, and we sailed off down the hall in a cloud of goodbyes. I couldn't believe this was happening to me. So fast. So newly out of bed. So against the rules.

Neither could a lot of the kids believe it. When we got outside to the car, a small group of them left the baseball diamond and approached us, jostling for a look at my father through the rolled down window, realizing, to their disbelief, that I was going to drive away with him.

"What you mean, you 'goin'...you *can't* go home from Bed Rest. Nobody go home from Bed Rest, girl..."

"I am, though, I guess," I said, my fingers trailing down the wooden side of the station wagon as it slowly pulled away. I was conscious of fixing an image of these kids in my memory while pieces of me strained both forward and backward. The knot of them stood stock still on the blacktop as our car moved down the long driveway.

Just before the hill dropped us out of sight I looked back and waved to the figures, still grouped together, now much smaller. They waved back, then they were gone. When the Hudson River appeared below us and we turned north along it, toward Maine, toward my wild summer heart, toward all that was dearest to me, I laid my head down in the open window and, inexplicably to my father, started to cry, hard.

Three years later I stood in the front hallway of Irvington House—a junior in high school. With Sam's help, I'd arranged to volunteer two afternoons a month. This was my first day.

A doctor greeted me in the hall.

"I'm very glad to meet you," he said, shaking my hand. "I've looked at your chart so many times since you were a patient here and still haven't figured out what you had. Neither has anyone else." I said that I was just glad the disease had disappeared, seemingly for good.

"I wish some other kids had been so fortunate," he said.

"What do you mean?"

He turned me around gently and walked me a little way down the hall. There were rows of bronze plaques on the wall, arranged by year of residence. It took me a minute to understand: these were names of children who had died. I felt as though I might throw up.

I couldn't imagine searching out the plaque for my

year and of course I was instantly compelled, with a bottoming out stomach, to do just that. And there it was, our plaque, our year, the names jumping out from the wall like stars on fire: Oscar...Buck... Ellen...Maria...Judy (Big Judy!)...Julio! Too many other names for me to register; too many faces jumbled together with shouts and laughter from voices now forever stilled. An unfamiliar bitterness rose in my throat.

I turned to the doctor, wanting to lash out—at him, at the plaques, at the universe—but I only croaked out the words, "What happened to them?"

He looked pensive. Echoing Sam, years before, he simply said, "We can only treat them while they're here and that's often not long enough. It's not followed by the care they need. We regret it terribly."

So this is what privilege looks like, I thought. Privilege goes home from Bed Rest, recovers on an island in Maine, returns in a few years as a volunteer. Privilege means having the chance to return at all.

The doctor made a move to draw me away from the wall. "Wait," I said. "There was a girl...she took special care of me...her name isn't here, so is she...?"

He looked particularly pained. "Lorraine?"

I nodded.

He pointed across the hall to another plaque with only one name. I moved toward it as though with fifty pound weights on my feet. My heart quailed on reading the inscription that honored Lorraine for the faithful care she gave to Irvington House children over many years. It sagged further to see she was only nineteen when she died. For the first time, I glimpsed the guilt-laced irony of knowing that someone I loved had died far too young—as I lived on into years they would never see.

The doctor waited a moment before he walked me over to a bench, suggesting I take a little time to sort out what I'd experienced. I tried to do this, but felt undone. Any sense of personal gratitude I'd begun to develop over the past few years was still tenuous. I wasn't old enough yet to understand that blessings and curses often spill from tributaries emptying into a single broad river.

Something I did understand, though, sitting in that hallway at sixteen, haunted by memories both dark and sweet: I was indeed rich. Rich beyond measure. And I understood one more thing, with an accompanying note of deep rue. My companions for a very short season, now ghosting along these walls, would never have guessed that my riches had anything whatsoever to do with them.

Coda

Almost twenty years after my stint at Irvington House as a volunteer, I edged my pickup truck along the familiar driveway. It was a gorgeous spring morning. The hulking Gothic building was as forbidding as ever, still crouched like an enormous stone lion looking down on the Hudson River.

Stepping from the truck, breathing in the sweet air of early May, I heard stray shouts and laughter, out of sight. I was aware this was no longer a hospital for children with rheumatic fever; it was now a home for delinquent kids. That didn't matter to me. Through a haze of déjà vu, the children I'd been here with felt very present, in one form or another.

Anticipation was making me sweat. I'd arranged to come see Mr. L., my social worker during the time I was a patient. He was still on the staff. My family thought it was odd of me, so many years later, to be making this journey; I knew it was necessary. I had some questions I'd never been able to shake. After entering the building, I was shown into a room where someone told me Mr. L. would come talk with me. And shortly he did.

I soon cut to the chase. "I want to know," I said, "whether you think it's possible I never had rheumatic fever at all but was experiencing some kind of strange, psychological reaction to my mother."

He looked at me long. And with a measure of affection that made me remember why I'd trusted him when I was young. "I don't know," he said. "I wondered at the time exactly what was going on with you."

"What do you mean?" I asked.

"Well," he said, "Your mother came to see me a couple of times during your stay here. I thought she was a pretty difficult customer. When you called last month and asked for this conversation with me, I looked back into the Irvington House records. I saw that even though you had many of the symptoms of rheumatic fever, the diagnosis was murky from the start." I told him that when I'd been a teenaged volunteer there, a doctor I encountered had voiced similar perplexity.

Mr. L and I talked at length, he very open about exploring why, over the years, I had experienced persistent uncertainty about what brought me to Irvington House. I told him that in addition to seeing him, I'd planned on this same trip to spend some time with the psychiatrist I'd gone to weekly during my junior year in high school. I explained that, these many years later, I was trying to pick up a number of seemingly disparate threads in my life, to make new sense of them in light of a recent searing divorce.

He was sympathetic and didn't find my return to this chapter of my life peculiar. At the end of our conversation he accompanied me to the hallway where I'd encountered the bronze plaques. He acknowledged them with a sad nod and then grasped both my hands in a warm goodbye, not needing to add that he was thankful my name wasn't on the wall.

I drove the truck down the driveway, looking back up at the building, as I had done on that day with my father so many years earlier. I knew I would never return; I'd retrieved the piece of myself I'd come for. I only wished that my father, now dead, were still at the wheel beside me, his large hand reaching for mine.

Same house. Same back yard. Same quiet suburban street. For an entire academic year I'd come here once a week after school to talk to a man who was saving my life— though I didn't know it at the time. Now, almost two decades later, I had begun to understand what he'd done for me.

As he opened the door, I suddenly felt as though I had four knees and that they were all about to buckle. He smiled at me. He looked out to the street, said, "Nice truck," and motioned me inside.

—☀—

Dr. V. was a psychiatrist located by my parents. He had a practice in our small town and came with a long list of impressive credentials, including lots of work with teenagers. He had a sterling reputation. I, however, didn't give a hang about his reputation; if he'd been the Man in the Moon I couldn't have been less disposed.

The circumstances that prompted my going to Dr. V. had mortified and infuriated me. In a nutshell: the summer preceding my junior year in high school I was involved with a guy on the island who was nine years my senior. Worried about the disparity between our ages and backgrounds, my parents were at their wits' end about this liaison and had employed a number of strategies to get me to end the relationship. I wouldn't. I was convinced of my own wisdom and smitten—with someone I experienced as loving and unfailingly kind. It had not occurred to me that my parents might have a superior corner on wisdom in this situation.

At the very end of the summer, my fate as a future patient of Dr. V.'s got sealed. Shortly after I crept into our cottage after the curfew hour one night, a harrowing scene erupted that involved my mother yelling, me crying and denying, and she waving aloft the thoroughly rumpled shorts and underclothes that I had (idiot!) left on the bathroom floor. The next morning, my parents decided I might be pregnant. I wasn't—I couldn't be—I hadn't engaged in the requisite behavior. That detail cut no mustard, however, and my mother declared that I, young lady, was destined for a counselor's office the minute we got back home.

In addition, the romance was pronounced over. No discussion. I left the island cocooned in heartache, making it plain to my mother she shouldn't *dare* to speak one word to me about this. I set my wrathful teeth against any counselor they might unearth, even though I knew I would eventually lose.

When I did land in Dr. V.'s office a few weeks later, I fought back by clamming up. I kept the appointments—but I wouldn't talk. This was partly because I was still nursing my lovelorn tantrum. More importantly, though, my parents had talked to Dr. V. before I met with him, and I didn't trust him not to relay to them—especially to my mother—everything I said.

Mired in mistrust, I had many expensive naps on Dr. V.'s therapy couch, and whiled away more than one hour on the swing in his back yard. Even when I accompanied him to his workshop in the basement below the office, I didn't say much—at least nothing consequential. Or so I thought. One day I spent the entire session feeling along his office walls for microphones, checking for taping equipment. He was amused by my overactive imagination, but let me search. He was unflaggingly patient, no doubt sure that at some point I would capitulate to his steadfastness. And, of course, I did. Mostly because he continued to promise, in tones I could finally believe, that our conversations were private. He said he'd made it plain to my parents that he was only willing to take me on if they agreed he would divulge nothing to them—short of my posing a danger of some sort. I never posed any such danger; he never talked to them. And eventually I fell for him like a ton of bricks...quite according to therapeutic plan, I much later understood.

Fast forward, as he invited me now into the same office, and perhaps to the same chair, where I had once majored in resistance to him. We spent some minutes navigating a few social niceties, adjusting to the weird sensation of time expanding and shrinking. I couldn't get over how old he looked, guessing he was in his early seventies. Perhaps he felt similarly about my being in my mid-thirties. He didn't say. He just seemed interested that I was there at all. He told me he'd never had a patient return after so many years. And he made it plain that—no matter why I'd come—he was very pleased to see me.

It is nearly impossible to describe how glad, how strangely relieved, I was to be in his presence again. Though it had been such a long time since I'd seen him, I reconnected very fast with the strength and wholeness and health he had signified for me.

As a teenager I hadn't understood just how life saving a figure Dr. V. was, but over the succeeding years a strong sixth sense about him emerged. I eventually saw that he had indeed snatched me, back then, from the jaws of serious emotional trouble. This realization didn't prevent me from continuing on in my career as the architect of my own destruction, especially my repeated downfall in matters of romance. By the time of this visit with him, though,

I did understand that long ago he had given me priceless psychological tools, and my gratitude to him for that was intense.

As that insight about his role in my mental health swept over me once again in his office, a Grand Coulee Dam of tears at last let go. What were those tears about? What complicated rivers of circumstance and sorrow set them rolling and gouging out their banks of muddy experience? Who knew...what mattered was the permission I still felt from him, stretching back over many years, to ride the tears to the bottom of the riverbed. He didn't question me. He waited. He murmured encouragement. And we inched ahead.

Over the following four days I saw him for an hour a day. We dug into why I thought my life was such a screwed-up mess, ferreting out a host of facts and feelings. We worked hard. And as we made our way forward, the other reason I'd come back to see him began to emerge. It was to hear him say I wasn't crazy now and I hadn't been crazy when I was sixteen. I needed reassurance that, despite what looked like a madly zigzagging path, there were deeper truths underneath the surface that caused all the twists and turns to make their own kind of sense.

On the last day I saw him, he told me that when I'd left his care at the end of my junior year, he had some lingering concerns about whether I was going to be okay. He deliberately hadn't conveyed those concerns to my parents. Instead, he said, he'd decided to trust that what we'd done together would eventually bear fruit and lead me to believe in myself.

"And what do you think now?" I asked. He gave me a smile I have carried in my emotional wallet ever since. "You are fine now," he said softly. And I believe you will *be* fine until the end of your life."

"Despite screw-ups, past and future?" I said.

"Screw-ups are never the point," he replied. "It's the strengths you bring to the task of untangling them."

When it came time to say goodbye, I felt a great desire to resist the departure, to extend the connection, to say something about seeing him again at a future date. As I might have guessed, that false move didn't have a chance. Standing at the front door with me, though, to hand me out to my truck, he looked at me with great gentleness when I asked if I might kiss him goodbye. He hesitated for just a millisecond before saying yes. And after I kissed his cheek he turned away quickly, but not before I caught a glimpse of his shining eyes.

The Green Bough

Though I didn't know it at first, the silence turned out to be the blessing. All I experienced as I initially settled into the retreat house was the disorienting fact of the silence — not its freedom.

One gray November morning in the mid 1970's, when I was enduring an equally gray marriage, I walked down to the corner store in the coastal Maine village where we lived and bought a copy of the New York Times.

Back home again, I sat down at my kitchen table with the newspaper and a cup of coffee. I soon noticed a story I would normally not have paid much attention to. It was about a small group of so-called "renegade" Roman Catholic nuns in upper New York State. I was not from a Catholic family myself, but I'd had Catholic childhood friends who hadn't fared well at the hands of nuns, so a lingering antipathy might have caused me to turn the page.

But I didn't. And as I read on in the article I realized that some distant region of my spirit was stirring. It was similar to the sensations I'd felt a couple of months earlier when I finished a novel called *In This House of Brede*, by Rumer Godden, about a powerful, strong-willed business-woman who kicks over the traces of her life and enters a Catholic women's religious order, eventually becoming an equally powerful and strong-willed nun. Unexpectedly, the book had captivated me.

The newspaper account described the banding togeth-er of this group of four or five women and the retreat house they had created in a suburb of Albany. Principally intent on a community designed to deepen their own spir-itual lives, they were also open to all sorts of women seek-ing short or extended periods of contemplation.

The nuns were teachers, social workers, school admin-istrators—some holding positions with a lot of authority—who had chosen to leave those jobs and take on work as domestics, thereby freeing up time and heart for prayer and various meditative practices. They were not defying the church hierarchy with this decision; their immediate superiors supported them. They nevertheless had some local detractors, cited in the article, who found their amal-gam of Eastern and Western traditions offensive. An ac-companying photograph showed the nuns dressed in jeans and work shirts sitting on the floor in front of a traditional Christian altar, described as engaged in Buddhist medita-tion. Back then, when religious observance was far more integrated into American life than it is today, not much explanation was needed to demonstrate why the term "renegade" might have stuck to these women and drawn some criticism. At the least, they were an iconoclastic bunch.

About as quickly as I read the article, I was flushed with a certainty I'd seldom experienced. I put down the newspaper, walked to the phone, and asked for the community's number in New York. I wasn't suddenly imagining I wanted to become a nun—far from it. I did realize, though, that for some time now I'd been half-consciously seeking somewhere to go on a spiritual retreat. I wanted a place where no one knew me, where I could explore some questions I had about God. And perhaps a place where I could face into my current marital unhappiness. Yes, this religious community was a long way from home. And yes, on the surface it was an unlikely haven for me. But it also seemed like an utterly right destination. When their phone began ringing I very much wanted them to say yes, come.

Six weeks later, as I crept along in my car in the descending dusk, through snow just beginning to blanket a suburban neighborhood, I came upon the place almost by accident. I had been anticipating a building with some sign that identified it as a retreat center. Instead, when I found the right number, I was in front of a house that looked like every other on the block. Perplexed, but relieved to finish the long trip, I hiked my stuff out of the car and approached the brightly lit front entrance.

I had barely knocked when a young woman opened the door. She said she'd seen the lights of my car, figuring it had to be me. As she swept me inside on a wave of friendly welcome, exclaiming about the snow, I stared at her, startled. Though I guessed she must be one of the nuns I'd come to stay with for a few days, she didn't look like any nun I'd ever seen. Dressed in old pants and a soft sweater, with curly hair framing a very pretty face, she told me her name was Clarice and flashed me a broad smile. Not Sister Clarice—just Clarice.

"No one else is home yet," she said, "and I didn't expect to be here myself to greet you. That's why we put the signs up for you this morning before we went to work."

It was then that I saw, on the wall in front of us, a homemade sign with a large arrow saying, "Mary! This way to your room." Nonplussed, I said, "But there wasn't any sign *outside* the house. You must have assumed I would just walk in..."

"Of course," she said, as she led me up a narrow set of stairs. This idea, that they had expected me to come into their house, a stranger, unaccompanied by any of them, set a wave of warmth coursing through me.

Another sign hung on the door at the top of the stairs, saying, "Mary! This is your room." Clarice opened the door, encouraged me inside. "Make yourself at home here and also down in the living room," she said. "Supper will happen soon after everyone's back from work." She smiled at me again and then withdrew without further conversation—a pattern I was to experience repeatedly during my time here: when all that needed saying had been said, there was no point in filling the air with extra talk.

The room was small, with a narrow bureau and a single bed. It was sparse but homey, with a faded hooked rug on the wooden floor. Except for bath towels draped over a rod, and a bedside lamp, there was only one piece of decoration: an appliquéd wall hanging, with a quote identified as a Chinese proverb: *keep a green bough in your heart and the singing bird will come*. I winced. It felt as though any green boughs in my heart had long since gone to brown, and I wasn't at all confident they could be grafted with new life. Singing birds seemed far off.

I put my clothes in the bureau and tried to fight a dual sensation of excitement and disorientation. Taking the book I'd brought from home, I ventured back down to the living room. Like my bedroom, its furnishings were simple although not austere. The floor was covered in wall-to-wall carpeting, a bunch of books were scattered around on various tables, and a few pictures hung on the walls. A crucifix was propped on one corner of a bookcase, a statue of Buddha on another. No one was around. I thought that Clarice must be causing the muffled sounds of meal preparation I could hear from the kitchen, but she didn't emerge. Delicious smells were filling up the house; the quiet of the evening felt fulsome, pregnant.

My own deteriorating mood was no match for the serene surroundings. I now was feeling faintly irritable, wishing someone would tell me what to expect. The certainty I'd felt about this venture while I was still in Maine was in danger of being swallowed by the thick silence of the place. I took comfort from the fire that was burning in the fireplace across from the couch where I sat, and my separation from the snow I could see sifting down against the window. But I wasn't relaxed.

Before long, a clatter came from the hall beyond the kitchen—the noise of people arriving through the front door. Oddly, however—or oddly to my ears—I heard no talk, no words of greeting, none of the chatter people normally make coming home after a day at work. Women straggled through the living room and moved toward the staircase, mostly taking no notice of me. A couple of them nodded at me on their way up the stairs, or smiled, but no one spoke. It seemed peculiar, awkward, without the usual padding that covers most human interaction. It wasn't unfriendly. It just felt...strange.

I kept reading my book for another 10 minutes or so, at which point the sisters began to reappear and gather in an adjoining room that I had guessed was a chapel. Still no instruction was forthcoming. And then, as though riding on some heaven-sent beam of light, Clarice came out of the kitchen and asked me whether I would like to join them for the evening meditation. In a jumble of relief and hesitation I followed her into the darkened chapel, stretching out on the floor as the others were doing, and waited to see what would happen. Outwardly, not much did. One of the sisters rang a small bell. All the energy in the room then seemed to collapse into quiet, accompanied only by the sound of sleet hammering hard now against the windows, and the occasional stomach gurgle.

After a few minutes, I realized that I had never experienced silence like the one that descended. It felt devoid of anxiety—except for my own—and even that gradually abated, as though displaced by something far more penetrating. Slowly, slowly, I allowed the darkness, the stillness, the smell of dinner, to envelop me. Until, lying there, a patch of impenetrability inside me began to melt. It wasn't that I "did" anything particular; it's more that I made room for something much larger than myself to take up residence. To put it another way: I let go of the unending internal monologue, my monkey brain, and settled back into simply listening.

At which moment it occurred to me, for the first time in my life, that prayer was perhaps mostly about listening—not speaking—and all about making interior space. At one point someone rang another bell, and we ended the meditation as unceremoniously as we'd begun it. I had no sense of how much time had passed, only that I'd been immersed in some sort of holy bath. As the greyness that had spurred this trip now started evaporating for real, I went in to supper with a renewed spirit.

I was unprepared, though, for what happened next. As soon as we sat down at the dining room table and one of the sisters offered grace, the five women erupted in a geyser of questions...where exactly did I live in Maine, and what was it like there, what did I do for work, did I have children. Taken aback by their eagerness to engage me, I saw that the reticence I'd felt from them earlier, when they'd arrived home from work, hadn't been reticence at all. The time for talk just hadn't arrived yet; now it was upon us full tilt.

And as it unfolded, it became complex, satisfying talk—as rich and resonant as the previous silence. All during supper and for the hour afterward lingering at the table, while they related their thoughts about work that day, and talked of their life in community and solicited reflections from me, I was struck by the complete absence of superficiality in the conversation. After a couple of the sisters waved away my attempt to help with the dishes, I climbed the stairs back up to my room thinking that a greening bough might be closer than I thought.

The following morning, a Saturday, I woke to more snow and the smell of bacon. As a surge of energy overtook me, I hustled into my clothes and was downstairs in about fifteen minutes, not wanting to miss anything.

I needn't have hurried. Without any talk among themselves or to me, the sisters were milling around in the kitchen as they fixed various versions of breakfast...and then they disappeared. I didn't understand. I wanted to ask, but didn't. Only a single piece of information from them came my way: the eggs in the bowl on the counter were hardboiled. Hearing no other news, I assembled some breakfast and took it over to the dining table. Once I sat down there, though, I realized that all the others must have gone into the living room. I felt unsure of myself, but decided to take my breakfast and go join them.

They were seated on the floor at a low round table, in front of a fire that was crackling away into a roomful of dense quiet. Seeing me approach, they each shifted slightly, making space for me to sit. A couple of them smiled at me.

Accompanied by the sounds of our eating, breakfast continued in companionable silence. And before long, I had a surge of comprehension. Of *course* no one had spoken to me back in the kitchen, or made suggestions about what to eat or where to eat it. They assumed I would figure it out for myself and do whatever I wanted. They knew, as I didn't, that maintaining the silence would free us, whereas inconsequential chat would bind us up. If I wanted eggs: fine. If I sat at the dining table: fine. If I joined them: fine. But if they gave me a roster of choices, it would just wrap invisible restraints around *my own* choices. Clearly, they preferred — and preferred to offer me — release from the prison that talk can construct. Without saying so, they had nevertheless said: there's no need for discussion, and whichever course of action you choose doesn't matter.

Simple as this may seem, it was a revelation. First of all, I hadn't been aware of how much I normally allowed anxiety to drive me into small talk. Secondly, prior to this moment I would have said silence was something to be filled; I didn't understand that certain kinds of silence were already full.

By *not* explaining anything, however, by *not* commenting, by keeping quiet, the sisters had signaled that my choices during my time with them were my business. The subtle warp and weft of their hospitality consisted of just this: to accept, to allow, to make room. In other words, to let be. In some theological circles, this is a definition of who God is—the one who lets be. I now understood that their purpose was to honor whatever needs I had by placing me in charge of meeting those needs.

This was a singularly liberating realization; it is also one that I've experienced in some similar guise in every monastic community I've visited in the succeeding forty years. It's an unarticulated invitation to figure out what customs are followed in that particular community. There is only a single unvarying requirement: *to respect the times and ways silence is observed and maintained.* Beyond that, one's choices about participation aren't important. It's a bit like being a fish swimming in a stream. Just as the stream doesn't "notice" the fish's presence, so a community of monks or nuns will not usually mark your arrival and departure or your inclusion in specific activities with any particular care or fanfare. Come, stay, go. Be welcome while you are here, and we won't take special notice when you leave. It's a bracing standard—carrying as much freedom as the stream does for the fish.

That standard surfaced again on Sunday morning when they brought me with them to a worship service at a community of Eastern Orthodox monks. After we all climbed into their van for the hour-long drive, it took me a few minutes to figure out that this was going to be a silent ride. I don't know why I had thought it might be otherwise—perhaps because of their infectious enthusiasm for the trip at a talking supper the night before. But then I remembered what I tended to forget: collective quiet was more often the norm for them than conversation. Understanding this, the silence in the car became full for me. Once I surrendered the expectation that we'd talk, I could sink into the conclusion that we wouldn't, and into the intense freedom that accompanied this conclusion. None of it felt awkward or unfriendly. And when the hour was over, instead of resisting the silence, I had now begun to crave its depths.

The counterpoint between silence and speaking continued to the end of my five days in the community. On the day before I left, I was sitting once again on the living room couch, reading, soaking up the rich peace of the house, when the sister who was the spiritual leader of the community came and stood next to me. She asked whether it would be helpful to talk. She said she'd noticed I sometimes seemed sad, but that she didn't want to intrude or barge unwanted into my solitude. I gratefully accepted her offer.

We ended up spending a long time together during which I revealed that, indeed, I was unhappily married to a severely depressed man and felt trapped—in part because I had been divorced once already as a much younger woman. Without a trace of judgment, she asked many tentative yet piercing questions. And with her in the lead, our conversation ranged from my anguish about a shadow of mortal illness then hanging over my father, to my current worry about soon re-entering college after the shame of flunking out more than a decade earlier, to sustaining a sex life within a context of marital bleakness and ongoing infertility. It hadn't occurred to me that this aging nun, with a history of life-long celibacy, would know the first thing about sexuality, or the heartache of infertility and childlessness. I had woefully underestimated her. Over and over she served up large cups of empathy, keen observation, and strong feeling—a brew of spiritual wisdom as bracing as black espresso.

At one point, she fixed her eyes on me with penetrating directness and said, "Do you imagine that the practice of celibacy is *any less complicated* than maintaining a satisfying sexual relationship?" The italics were hers. As we brought our conversation to a close soon after that question, she turned a deeply compassionate smile on me, took my hand in hers, and said, "You know, I think you might need to start asking whether God intends you to have a few flowers growing in your yard. If those flowers really can't be found in this marriage, then my sense is you may need to be elsewhere, difficult as it is for you to contemplate what looks like a second failure. The failure may be the entryway to a very different kind of success." And with that she left me to myself—full to the brim, and also curiously, wonderfully, empty. Somewhere, in a clearing now not so far off, I was sure I could detect a distinct note of birdsong.

A Flash of Saffron

The road to the Zen monastery curls through the Catskill Mountain greenery like a thick black snake. After leaving Route 17, which shoots on westward toward Ithaca, the trek up through the hills to the monastery is another twenty-five miles. And with each disappearing mile the landscape grows increasingly deserted: few houses, fewer cars, an occasional empty crossroad.

I made this trip four or five times in the late 1970's and early 1980's, on each occasion toting a backpack stuffed with conflicted feelings. Being at the monastery was a profoundly appealing prospect to me, and fit into my burgeoning desire for a deeper spiritual life. However, on driving into the parking lot, I also tended to plummet into resistance — tempted to do a quick turnaround and hightail it back home to Maine. The building itself, with its graceful Japanese architectural lines, the shimmering lake it's perched above, the dense woods surrounding it, all constitute a study in elegant isolation that both appeals and disturbs.

Which makes sense. The whole place is magnetic *and* forbidding, like any place where people have intentionally sought to penetrate the mystery of how God—in the infinite ways one might define God—is at work in their lives. And as with most spiritual communities, this one sparks a standard response to the numinous, to the divine: it simultaneously attracts and repels. So it was with me. Each time I arrived, as I turned the iron ring attached to the heavy wooden door that opened into the monastery and pushed on its dark bulk, I heaved a sigh that was part eager anticipation, part dread.

On one of my last trips there I was exhausted from the eight-hour car ride, and went soon to my bedroom for a nap, surfacing only when the familiar boom of the huge bronze gong behind the monastery resounded through my sleep. I knew this gong was the signal to come to the zendo, the meditation hall, for the sitting that would precede the evening meal. Quickly I put on the ankle length homespun robe I'd collected on arrival and slipped barefoot into the corridor beyond my bedroom door. Abandoning any pretense to mindfulness, I sprinted upstairs to the zendo, wanting to avoid the disapproving notice drawn by latecomers.

Unless one is brand new to this particular Zen monastery, no directions accompany the sitting—called zazen. I knew from previous visits, however, to claim an unoccupied tatami mat and small, round zafu, or pillow, arrange the robe around my knees as I knelt, and quiet my ragged breathing. It didn't take long. All of the rice paper windows lining the zendo had been opened wide to the evening, in effect bringing the outside in: falling light, pungent forest floor, rain dripping from the curved eaves. As the outlines of nearby trees sharpened in the gathering darkness, like an Eliot Porter photograph come to life, a welcome sense of familiarity erased the remaining traces of resistance. I was back.

In a few minutes, ten or twelve other people had settled near me on their knees or in yoga positions, on mats in two facing rows. The monk in charge of the sitting struck a small brass bowl, filling the hall with a chime that echoed off in fading rings and eventually died out in the trees beyond. Soon the sound of wood being knocked on wood reverberated from just outside the zendo, in a sequence that began slowly and increased in pace and intensity until a last sharp knock fell and the echo, again, passed away into the woods. The sitting had begun.

For the next half hour, with little stirring of limbs, we remained in our positions. There was no chanting, just layers of silence. Discomfort came and went without much murmur; I guessed that others, like me, knew the only way to deal with pain in our backs and bent legs was to acknowledge it, allow it to move through us, and let it go.

Toward the end of the sitting I became aware of something I hadn't experienced on any previous visit: a figure was moving down the other side of the zendo, walking slowly behind the opposite row of sitters. Despite the near-dark, I could see that it was a short, slight man, dressed in a skimpy shift ending at his knees. He had a shaved head; I assumed he was a monk. He carried a stick in one hand—the length and type of an old-fashioned primary school ruler. Trying unsuccessfully not to watch him, I saw him stop behind a woman and tap his stick on her shoulder. It wasn't a harsh tap; still, she straightened her back. He continued down the line, pausing occasionally to administer a similar light tap on a shoulder, a head, an upturned foot. He then moved past the open door at the front of the zendo and started walking behind my row. I was both hypnotically focused on him and anxious about being singled out. He didn't pause at my mat but did stop behind a couple of sitters to my right. Finally, he walked slowly out of the zendo, as light on his feet as the faint scent of incense that filled the room.

Going to supper a short time later, I asked one of the monastery's resident monks about this man. The look that crossed his face was a mix of bemusement, mischief, and wariness. "Did he smack you with his stick?" he asked.

"No," I said, "but I worried that he might. Actually, he didn't 'smack' anybody—just firmly tapped. His presence was a little unnerving, though."

"That's S. Roshi," the monk said, "E. Roshi's teacher from Japan. He's visiting with us for a while in order to spend time with E. Roshi. He will give all of us a teaching after supper. He speaks only extremely broken English, so pay attention to his actions instead of his words. You will probably learn from him without being aware you are learning anything at all."

My interest piqued, I went in to supper. I knew that E. Roshi, the abbot of the monastery, had come to the United States about ten years earlier to establish this Zen community and its "parent" organization in New York City. I hadn't had much interaction with him, but whenever I ended up in his presence I became keenly aware of his authority. If S. Roshi was his teacher, I assumed *his* authority was even greater.

As it turned out, S. Roshi delivered a lesson almost immediately—at supper. Eating at the monastery involved a complicated ballet with a set of graduated black lacquered bowls given to each retreatant at the first meal taken. The nested bowls were wrapped in a cloth napkin, stored in a cubbyhole outside the dining room, to be retrieved at the start of a meal, replaced at the finish, and kept for the duration of one's retreat. As directed by a monk, we were to make as little noise as possible when using the bowls. That was a nice theory; in reality, when in motion the bowls tended to clack. Loudly. Any eating, in other words, created a symphony of noises that everyone was attempting not to make—to the accompaniment of ringing silence.

S. Roshi, surely a longtime juggler of similar bowls in like settings, made short work of these constraints. With a boisterous flourish, he unwrapped the napkin enclosing his set of bowls. After joining the ritual offer of a token amount from the food we were all about to eat, he then romped through supper with gusto—filling the silence with great smacking of lips, satisfied grunts, and bowl clacking, ignoring the rest of us as we furtively watched him and kept on eating to the tune of the rules. E. Roshi sat opposite him and smiled widely through it all; at one point he clapped his hands in great glee. One lesson, at least, was clear: some rules were made to be broken. At least by S. Roshi.

After supper and a brief break (mostly for cigarettes; in the late 1970's smoking was frowned upon at the monastery but tolerated, so a bunch of us went outside and endured the frowns) we all reconvened on the floor of the dining room for the promised teaching. Some of the other retreatants had encountered S. Roshi before, as had the resident monks, which was probably why an air of expectation hovered over the room as each roshi entered. E. Roshi settled himself cross-legged on the floor; S. Roshi stayed standing, leaning on a cane as gnarled as he was. He trained a gimlet eye on us for a couple of minutes. And then, without preamble, seemingly apropos of *nothing*, he burst into peals of laughter that rolled out of him like church bells down a long, wide valley.

Something in me wanted to bolt. Not because his laugh carried the faintest whiff of malice or disapproval—it didn't. It was one of the merriest, most unguarded, full-of-delight sounds I'd ever heard. But it unnerved me in the same instant that it thrilled me, the way an open cell door might unnerve a prisoner. If someone could laugh that freely, what else might he do? I stayed put.

S. Roshi began walking around the room. Prancing was more like it. His saffron shift swayed with each movement of his body, and his bare feet seemed to float. He punctuated many of his steps with a noise that married a cackle and a hoot. Part elderly man, part boy, all dancing gnome, his reed-like body soon shook again with laughter that seemed to issue from beyond time and space—laughter that invited the rest of us to come out and play.

I was the first to crack. There was something so absurd about his mincing around while the rest of us sat in spellbound silence; I finally couldn't stop the laugh that was rising from my belly to my throat. Up it came and out it leapt: choked, but irrepressible. He stopped walking, turned to face me from across the room, and worked his hands vigorously, as if calling me, saying, *yes, yes, that's it, that's it, keep it coming, more, more, keep it coming*...until pretty soon I was laughing uncontrollably, at nothing and everything, at all things constipated, at every pretense of my own ego, at every pretense, period.

S. Roshi jumped in the air. "Ya, *ya!*" he yelled, or something like it, now egging everyone else on with his madly beckoning arms and his waving cane, like an insane conductor trying to tune up an even more insane orchestra, until the room was engulfed by a tsunami of roaring laughter, making most of us grip our sides and roll around on the floor. It made no sense at all, and I don't think I've ever spent three minutes in a scene that made *more* sense—absurd as it would have looked to a passerby. It was as though S. Roshi had released an emergency brake, a brake the rest of us hadn't even known existed, and by releasing it took us on a ride straight into the arms of glory. The resident monk had been right: we needed to ignore the broken English and listen for something else.

There was no explication following this, no hammering the lesson home. And a good thing. Any talk would have ripped through the moment like an unconscious body striding through a spider web. Instead, S. Roshi made a bow from the waist, stood to beam at us all, and vanished—leaving behind a saffron-colored exclamation point.

I experienced S. Roshi only once more during my visit. The following evening, when the gong sounded for meditation, he joined a number of us gathered outside for a round of meditative walking called kinhin. We were all in our robes, barefoot. Intended to counter long stationery periods of sitting in the zendo, the kinhin "procession" occurred on wooden walkways built around the outside walls of the monastery for this purpose. The single-file procession also wound through the long inside hallways; a monk at the head of the line slipping into the building and outside again—never breaking step or shifting tempo. Besides being welcome movement for stiff body parts, kinhin also had its own fast-paced appeal. And if the weather was blustery, as it was on that night, the wind in the treetops beat a syncopating rhythm with our slapping feet and the high-flying moon, exhilarating our spirits.

S. Roshi assumed no special role in the kinhin; he simply fell in with the rest of us. Once we got underway, though, his capacity *to be present to the moment and all that was in it* struck me as entirely singular. His intensity was deep, private, and somehow also open to the rest of us. Walking close behind him, listening to his feet hit the wood with such verve, I felt as though he were experiencing the wind and the walkway and the whipping trees as animate fellow participants. It struck me that he was piercing into some primal layer of existence, where all the disparate aspects of reality are bound together into something transcendent, something greater than just themselves.

What exactly is that "something greater?" No one can say because no one knows. In the moment, though, S. Roshi seemed to incarnate a glimpse into the heart of real religious impulse: ferociously attractive and powerfully scary. Just as in his laughter of the evening before, and the fire of laughter he lit in the rest of us, so too now in the quality of his presence on that walk, life itself came roaring out. His vitality seemed bottomless, a blessing so strong I could almost taste it. Which is perhaps one reason why, though he is now well beyond thirty years dead, some trace of his spirit can still surge in me...lofting his gnarled cane, rollicking through eternity.

Seen and Unseen

It started at the Isabella Stewart Gardner museum in Boston, not long after Tom and I were married in the mid-1980's. We were wandering among the museum galleries, marveling at the art collected there, when at one point we drifted apart and I ended up in a room looking at a wooden statue of a woman. If she hadn't been so small, I'd have guessed she was a figurehead carved for a ship. She was canted forward, her back pressed against a narrow, curved spar resembling a ship's prow. Her eyes, also, seemed outsized and focused intently downward, as though she were scanning the sea below for signs of trouble.

I studied this statue for a long while, admiring the delicacy of the craftsmanship, the rich sheen of the rose gold paint on the woman's cheeks and the faded cream and blue folds of her back-streaming skirt. The legend on the wall offered scant information, saying simply: *13th century Italian woodcarving. Unknown artist.*

Aware at one point that I'd lost track of Tom, I started

to leave the gallery to look for him. After a few steps, I suddenly felt a strong pull back toward the figure, as if I were magnetized.

I returned to the statue. After lingering for a minute, I again went to leave, this time getting as far as the gallery door opening, when I was once more gripped by a sensation of deep attraction. I went back to the carving a second time, distinctly unnerved.

Making myself walk away, I passed into an adjacent room and looked at a number of other statues and paintings. On a half-hearted search for Tom, and mentally at war with myself, for the third time I experienced the same force. There was no voice, no drama. Nevertheless, the propulsion to return remained strong and powerful, almost like a hunger. Fully spooked now, I did return—determined to break whatever spell this was.

I was only partly successful. Exiting the room one more time, I had to will myself to erase the former sensation from my consciousness and decide to ignore it if it reappeared. It did—faintly. When I found Tom and relayed this experience, he wanted to see the figure himself. We went back together, me with definite trepidation. Although he admired the beautiful carving, he was wholly unmoved; I felt only a hint of the former magnetism. Soon afterward we left the museum and I dropped the entire episode into Boston Harbor.

Four days later a follow-on event occurred, beginning in

the early morning while Tom and I were still asleep. In some circles, the experience would be called a "waking dream"—whatever it was, it landed on my psyche four-square, like an emotional line squall, and brought me upright in bed. Now roused from sleep, Tom turned to me and asked what was wrong.

"Do you remember the statue of the woman at the Gardner museum, the one that looked like a figurehead, that I couldn't seem to get enough of?" He remembered.

"Well, it sounds strange, but I intuitively know from a dream I just had that I've got some connection to the man who carved that statue. I don't think I'm a model for the figure, but I am someone in his life. I don't understand what it's about. The dream was as real as everything in this bedroom."

Tom knew I wasn't drawn to any kind of occult thinking; he asked to hear more.

"There's a second dream," I said, even as I realized that, although I was talking to him, I was still in a not-fully-awake state. He somehow understood this, eased me back down in the bed and quietly said, "Tell me the second dream."

"In it there's a filmy, almost gossamer curtain drawn across a small opening that looks like a stage for a puppet show. A narrow space exists between the two halves of the curtain and I feel powerfully drawn to that space—just the way I felt drawn to the statue of the woman."

I talked to him about the fear the dream held for me. I said that as I parted the curtain, and stuck my left leg over the lip of the stage, my heart was pounding while I attempted to maneuver my whole upper body through the opening. It was too small; I stopped. I explained to him what I experienced as I peered through the opening.

"There's a deep silence on the other side", I said. "It's a ringing silence, very full. I can see, not far from the opening in the curtain, a row of trees alongside a river. Their branches are being tossed by wind I can't hear. The banks of the river are well defined and the water moves along the banks at a glacial pace."

I tried to describe the human beings I saw on the surface of the water. They were packed close together, in some sense "buoyed up." They had faces and seemed to be all ages. Some wore white shrouds. They were like a "river of souls" gliding by, at rest on top of the water.

"As the dream goes on," I tell him, "I have a very strong desire to plant my whole self on the other side of the curtain, to reach the river. I try once more to push myself through the small stage opening. Without hearing any words, I experience a clear "no." It's an unmistakable warning to stop and to withdraw my leg. I definitely don't want to do that, but this is not a debate: it's plain I don't belong on the far side of the stage opening. I pull my leg back and the curtain brushes against my leg. It's over. The end of the dream leaves me with a feeling of enormous reassurance, a strong sense of loving 'care' specifically directed at me, and also great loss.

Tom was quiet when I finished. Now fully awake, lying in his arms, I asked what he thought it meant. Of the two of us, he was the one who'd had powerful spiritual experiences. He did not tend to talk about them publicly because such accounts usually provoked cynicism rather than curiosity.

"Tell me what *you* think it meant," he said.

"It seemed like a vision of the afterlife, or at least one aspect of it," I said. "It felt connected to the first dream about the maker of the statue and to the experience at the museum. Saying that, though, makes me feel a little unhinged. I'm completely baffled about how any of this can exist alongside everything else that I can see right here, right now."

That string of occurrences, which I view as one numinous event, happened more than thirty years ago. It remains as vivid for me now as it was then. I'm still not sure how all of it fits together, but in the succeeding decades nothing has dislodged my conviction that, despite all rational skepticism, I did somehow slip briefly through a crack in the cosmic egg. I can't prove this, of course. But I'm not much concerned with proofs. I can't prove the existence of God, either, but that doesn't stop me from living as though God is real.

Indeed, God started to *become* newly real for me as a result of these two oddly fused experiences. Prior to them, I'd have described myself as a believer in God, but a wary one. Now, though, sure that I hadn't lost my grip back there in the museum or in the subsequent dreams, I was equally sure that I had somehow accessed another reality. There was too much unusual energy, too much emotional power and "realness" for it not to be so. I experienced that realness as plainly as I experienced myself having two arms and two legs. I also saw that I had been rendering God much too small and limited. The experience radically enlarged my sense of God—from the inside out. Perhaps most importantly, I became conscious that I had been making a false distinction between what we can see and what we can't, assigning each to separate and unconnected spheres.

After the experience, I could understand the meaning of an ancient religious paradox: that the seen and the unseen are two aspects of one reality, both equally real and in tension with one another. Modern physicists would have no problem with this paradox. It is also not "news" to people of various religious persuasions; on the contrary, it is daily bread for many. But for me at the time, it removed a veil. Up until then, as a card-carrying member of the ultra-rational world, I had largely dismissed what I couldn't see. I paid lip service to the provinces of the unseen, but I assigned no true value to any treasure that might be buried there.

I don't know what happened to me while staring at the statue, or in being repeatedly drawn back to it, or in the succeeding dreams—I only know *that* something happened. And this "something" proved to be a distinct blessing, tipping me into new trust in whatever lies beyond material reality. The tension between what we can see and what we can't wasn't resolved; I don't think it's meant to be. But my relationship to that tension shifted and I felt as though I'd somehow been granted dual citizenship in the countries of the seen and the unseen.

The blessing lay in shedding a perspective that barred me from God—who is, arguably, the primary inhabitant of those "provinces of the unseen." God still remained enigmatic for me, as is the case for most people who concern themselves with such reflection. From that experience onward, though, God did feel accessible in new ways. No instant "Aha!" flung me into the arms of the Holy Spirit, but I felt a discernible change: as though an optometrist had been testing my vision with a multiple-lens device and clicked on a clearer lens.

Here's an elementary example of this change. Before the experience, if someone had told me a coffee table was a mass of vibrating atoms *that we have mutually agreed to call a table*, I would have scoffed. Yoked firmly to faith in my own five senses, I'd have insisted the table was indubitably solid and static in the bargain. After the experience, I realized that the truest "reality" of the table lay in motion I couldn't see. My five senses now weren't "all there is," but instead seemed like a foretaste of whatever mysteries are gathered beyond our ordinary sight. Clearly, accounting for what is unseen doesn't require a spiritual explanation—that same physicist can spring to the fore with a scientific explanation of the invisible vibrating atoms and be fully correct. My faith in unseen realms, however, while not at all dismissive of the science, now felt grounded elsewhere.

One other shift occurred as a result of this experience: my former fear of death abated. The fear didn't disappear, but it was pushed from center stage by curiosity and a kernel of conviction that hadn't existed before. If the ever-in-motion atoms of a table are its deepest truth, after all, and would remain so even if the table were burned to a crisp and rendered invisible, who is to say what happens to the atoms-of-us when we die and can't be seen any-more?

That altered perspective assumed a new importance for me when, a few short months after the museum/dream experience, Tom and I began a joint three-year seminary education. The decision to go to seminary wasn't connect-ed to the experience; it was a plan we embarked on a cou-ple of years earlier and had done a great deal of life reordering to make happen. We had also both been ap-proved as potential candidates for ordained ministry in the Episcopal Church. Despite the arduous path required to gain this approval, however, and my abiding thirst for spiritual inquiry and formation, I wasn't completely confi-dent in what I was doing when we arrived at seminary. I still had only a fledgling sense of how God was at work in my life and, at least outwardly, I wasn't an obvious candi-date for ministry.

I came from a family that was far more at home—in temperament as well as, in my father's case, employment—in the seats of a Broadway theatre than in the pews of a church. I had been nominally brought up in the Episcopal church of the late 1950's, but my tenure there ended with the onset of puberty and my parents' exasperation over the inevitable Sunday morning dawdle. Besides, they preferred staying home to read, except, perhaps, on Easter and Christmas, the high holy days of the functionally irreligious. As for me, primping in front of a large mirror was, by age twelve, a far more absorbing pastime than almost anything else, most especially the prospect of church.

It was a bit perplexing, then, roughly twenty-five years beyond my pubescent rejection of church, to be ranging around the ivied walls of Yale Divinity School. My mind was stuffed with questions. For starters, the background I brought felt like a disjointed fit with the vocational choice of ministry. I also had concerns about God, Christianity, and my roster of doubts. Our sponsoring Episcopal bishop in Maine, who'd clapped me on the back and proclaimed he'd vastly prefer "one fiery doubter to a hundred lukewarm clergy," was convinced I would thrive—in seminary and afterward in parish life. I wasn't so sure. As it turned out, Tom and I eventually did end up in long, lively ministries with skeptics and all sorts of tepid believers as well as with the high-spirited devout. But I didn't know that at the start.

I did have one speedy realization. As our first semester in seminary progressed, theological study felt completely disconnected from the singular authenticity of the museum/dream experience of a few months beforehand. I also understood that if I ventured out into the seminary community with an account of that experience, I would likely be met—at best—with raised eyebrows. In seminaries everywhere, of course, the existence of God is presumed. There is, in other words, *acknowledgement* of the unseen. But main line divinity schools are as steeped in rationalism as the culture at large and aren't necessarily receptive to student field reports. William Blake's actual visions (despite the enduring attraction of his art) would almost certainly be deemed way beyond the pale.

The fault line between my brief sojourn through the cosmic crack and my seminary education eventually widened into a crevasse. I still felt tremendously blessed by the former experience—I just carried it quietly, tucked away as a powerful source of strength. I'm not discounting all that I needed to study and practice in order to become a parish priest; I would have been a dismally poor handmaiden without the rigorous preparation I received at seminary. And eventually the book learning and the prior sense of blessing merged. During all the years of ministry to follow, however—whether burying stillborn babies or joining indomitable eighty-year olds in marriage—that long ago ineffable experience was my deepest source of living water.

The entire encounter carried a fierce authority. My previous faith in God, though somewhat fickle, had kept me moving for years on my own spiritual quest. But that faith had not yet turned into bedrock. After the experience, a kind of unshakeable certainly took over, an intuition that didn't budge. It was only *my* intuition, which rendered it unexplainable as well as inarguable. But for me it stood as confirmation that God's presence was as true as the sun, the moon, and the stars. Over many succeeding years this certainty continued to color my consciousness as indelibly as permanent ink, becoming a vital necessity for the singularly arduous work to come—in the following sense.

Pastoral ministry brings its practitioners into the presence of extraordinary joys and also smack up against some of the harshest brutalities life can deliver: agonizing illness, untimely death, unrelenting emotional challenges arising from everyday life. And the chief capacity a priest or pastor brings to those joys and woes is *the ability to embody the boundless love of an unseen God.* Try that out, though, in an anguished Emergency Room, tending the parents of a four-year-old sliced nearly in half by a hit-and-run driver. *Boundless. Unseen. Love.* It's a belief, a trust, so divorced from present day reliance on what is tangible, rational, clear, and visible as to come from another universe. Yet that trust is what's required for any ministry worthy of the word.

Clergy need to be able to move fluidly between those visible and invisible universes. But immediately the problem becomes clear. Not only is the unseen world mostly disregarded, it is also mostly impossible to talk about *because* it's unseen. It may be no less real, but because its "realness" is at best elusive it's easy to dismiss. Think of the oft-heard response to dreams, when a listener will say, "Oh, it's just a dream," meaning there's no need to give it any real weight. The ephemeral nature of a dream, its van-

ishing-ness, its *unseen-ness,* tends to render it about as sub-
stantial as fairy dust—and as likely to be taken seriously.
That lack of serious engagement leads, though, to profound loss, because dismissing dreams or other unseen
aspects of our experience shuts the lid on large coffers of
emotional, intellectual, and spiritual riches.

The alternative to our dismissiveness is to accept that
the realness of the unseen can only be hinted at. In this it's
like grace. Grace may be the most prominent feature of our
lives—I daresay none of us draws a breath without it—and
yet *we have to take it on faith that grace exists at all.* It surely
doesn't "exist" in the sense that a coffee table does. But
would the table have ever come together if grace had not
been present in all the influences that produced the soil
that produced the tree that produced the wood and produced the hands that eventually created it? Grace always
comes to us sideways, indirectly, like a melody playing
from unseen quarters.

This sideways nature of grace points to one of the
chief difficulties in talking about God. God is always discernible only in sideways glimpses, in contrast to the realness of a concrete object. The "realness of God" is more
like the light of the silvery moon. That light is evident, but
we can't catch a moonbeam any more than we can catch
strains of music coming from an indeterminate source.
God is similarly elusive, like the "glimmering girl" in W.B.
Yeats' "Song of Wandering Aengus," who calls the poet's
name and then flits away through an enchanted wood,
forever evading, laughing, leaving behind only the scent of

the apple blossoms tucked in her hair. God is like that: there and not there, always maddeningly around the next bend — and driving us around the bend in the bargain.

Does this mean God can't be counted on? Not at all. But it does mean that whatever "counting on" we do has to be of a wholly different order from the visible one we are accustomed to...the kind of order one might glimpse through two halves of a gossamer curtain. Or might hear shining out of the ancient story about the rabbi who said to the almond tree, "Speak to us of God," and the almond tree burst into flower.

Spiritual teachers have always known that we human beings need help to trust in what will forever remain beyond our sight. That is, after all, a principal purpose of spiritual practice — to remind us, repeatedly, that unseen realities are as real as what is seen. But as modern-day rationalists, such trust is very difficult for us. The process of gaining it runs hard against the powerful current of our Show Me, Prove It tendencies. And yet isn't this also true: so much of what we feel most strongly about, like our deep gratitude for the blessings in our lives, can never literally be shown or proven. Could I have "proven" the force I felt emanating from that little carving in Boston? Never. And yet it has accompanied all my subsequent footsteps with its strange and wonderful shadow. Perhaps the most faithful course we can follow is to acknowledge that all blessings contain *both* the seen and the unseen, and then live into the complexity of embracing each realm with equal ardor.

Sister, Sister

The first time I heard Mr. Esposito, he was calling for a nurse to bring him water. He was a patient on one of my assigned wards at the large urban hospital where I was in chaplaincy training. As I walked past his door I heard him change his cry for water to "Sister, Sister!" He was now calling me and, for reasons unknown, had apparently decided I was a nun. Gathering my un-nun-like mental skirts around me, I tentatively approached him.

I had avoided this room. One week earlier, at the start of the chaplaincy program, I learned that Mr. Esposito had pancreatic cancer and probably wouldn't live long. This was the disease that had claimed my own father a decade earlier, and the memory of that loss still had some power to undo me. I was keen to sidestep any reminders. And now the reminder was right in front of me; far more up close and personal than I wanted, but there was no getting around it—I was a chaplain, after all, or imitating one. I pulled up a chair.

Mr. Esposito's rangy, seventy-year old body was topped by a swarthy, dark-eyed face framed with a mass of curly black hair: one hundred percent Italian American. His splayed fingers on well-worn hands suggested a long life of labor. Now, all his labors done, he clearly expected death to come around the corner any minute and speak his name. Intermittently he fought with a surge of pain.

He reached for my hand, then squeezed it hard.

"I know I don't have much time," he said. "I know I'm dying. You're a Sister, aren't you?" he asked.

"I'm not," I said. "I'm a chaplain in training."

"Well, I don't care who you are," he said. "Chaplain, Sister, it's all the same to me. I haven't been to church, or confession, in over forty years and I need someone to hear my confession *now,* and to pray me out of this life."

Hear a confession? Formally? I had no experience in doing that. 'Pray him out'? Not likely I could do a credible job. Suddenly all the fears of the preceding week came crashing down on me—fears that I was in the wrong room, on the wrong train, maybe on the wrong planet. My name-tag said *chaplain,* but for days I'd had the feeling that I was meant to take it off, pin it on someone else.

"Mr. Esposito," I said, my anxiety rising, "Aren't you a Roman Catholic?" I rushed on without waiting for his reply. "Wouldn't you like me to find you a priest?" He winced. "I'm a Catholic, all right," he said, in a voice layered with embarrassment and bitterness. "A very bad Catholic. That's why I don't want no priest. I want you."

All week long, since starting this training, I'd been skulking in various obscure corners of the building thinking that if I could only locate the right closet, I'd find a suit of clothes hanging there that would turn me into a chaplain. So far, all those closets had been empty. And now, in the room of this dying man, I realized there wasn't going to be any magic closet or chaplain-sized suit of clothes. Instead, God's gloriously peculiar sense of humor was going to arrange my rescue through someone even more at his wit's end than I was. There might as well have been a sign over Mr. Esposito, flashing NO EXIT. Swallowing the irony, I closed the door to his room and sat down again.

It was then that I spied the small, thin, black book on his bedside table. I couldn't believe what I was seeing. It was The Pocket Book of Prayer, something Tom's grandfather, a beloved and formidable Methodist bishop, had compiled many decades earlier. I picked it up and asked Mr. Esposito whether it was helpful to him. He looked at me doubtingly and said, "Are you kidding? I read that thing every day. I never go to church, but that little book always helps me, soothes me." I told him my connection to it and he was flabbergasted. "I knew you were the one I wanted", he said, "not some Catholic priest. What more proof do you need that you were supposed to come into my room?"

And then, without much additional preamble, we set to work. Having little clue what I was doing, I encouraged him to speak of anything he felt badly about, to just fling his transgressions out into the room and offer them up to

God. Which he did—with more confessional fervor than I have encountered in anyone since. He blurted out the ways he'd failed his kids, the smacking around of his wife, his anger at his in-laws, his sexual infidelities. It went on without letup, sins large and small: his laziness, his pride, his sense of superiority...shaming his teenaged daughter, letting his father win at cribbage, being overly critical of his son's baseball playing. This extended litany, keenly felt, was full of emotional pain. At the end of it, he lowered his head onto his drawn-up knees and sobbed like a seven-year-old.

After a long pause I said, "I want to do something I'm technically not supposed to do."

"What is it?" he asked.

"I want to give you a blessing," I said, "for your bravery."

"Bravery?" he asked. "This feels like bravery to you?"

"It sure does. And even though I'm supposed to be ordained before blessing someone, at the moment I care more about what seems right than I do about the rules."

"Do anything you want," he said. "I figure I need all the blessings I can get. Can you also give me absolution?"

"Not technically."

"Ask me if I care about technically," he replied.

At that point, I took his hands in mine, descended into a completely unfamiliar zone in myself, and began a prayer that was part blessing, part absolution, all fox hole. I could feel him responding, first through his hands. And then he too began to pray aloud, alongside my words, and all in a rush the Holy Spirit took over. I pressed my high heels so hard into the linoleum floor that I nearly wore grooves in it. He began to cry again and soon the tears were cascading down my own cheeks. This went on for a couple of minutes until, just as I was thinking justice might roll down like water and righteousness like an ever-flowing stream, our prayers stopped as quickly as they had begun, and the waters—of all sorts—abruptly subsided.

I wasn't sure what to do next. Mr. Esposito had fallen back against his pillows; I wondered whether our mutual Pentecostal seizure had done him in. Then he opened his eyes.

"I don't know how to thank you," he said. "I knew I needed this, but I really didn't know how much."

"Well," I said, "I have to tell you that any thank-you runs both ways. It might surprise you to hear it, but this is the first time since I came to the hospital that I thought I might be doing some good. I felt pretty useless twenty minutes ago."

A smile flushed his cheeks and creased his handsome Roman nose. He looked half his age.

"You'll do good," he said.

I stayed a few more minutes, and then, seeing that a wave of pain was enveloping him again, withdrew, promising to pray for him, as he'd asked.

Although I did stop by Mr. Esposito's room over the next

few days, and he seemed glad enough to see me, he actually wasn't much interested in my being there. It was clear to me too: since we'd accomplished the necessary deed, all else was superfluous. Besides, because he was in increasing pain, visitors were a problem. Members of his large family often bunched up in the hallway outside his room and, except for the hospital's Roman Catholic chaplain, they didn't invite interruption. I stiffened slightly whenever I saw the priest entering or leaving the room, knowing as I did a little about the man in the bed beyond the door, but it was hardly a moment for umbrage—even hidden.

The last time I saw Mr. Esposito was by chance. He was lying on a hospital gurney in an elevator, being taken downstairs for discharge to die at home. When I spoke to him as I stepped into the elevator he didn't recognize me; he was heavily sedated. As the aide accompanying him maneuvered the gurney for exit on the ground floor, I asked him to stop. Faintly impatient, he nevertheless braked the gurney and nodded at me with an indulgent smile while I made the sign of the cross on Mr. Esposito's forehead. The aide knew this was just something certain chaplains sometimes felt they needed to do.

The Eloquence of Mr. B.

"But since he had the stroke eleven years ago, he hasn't spoken a word," said the charge nurse, her tone eclipsing further discussion. It was obvious: a pastoral visit with Mr. B. didn't make much sense to her.

I buried a surge of irritation. Suppressing my own fears about Mr. B's inability to talk, I pasted on a smile and asked her to point me in the direction of his room. "401, down at the end of that hall." As I walked away from the nursing station, she called after me, in a lilt that announced she was pleased to be in the know, "He probably won't be there. He rides around in his wheelchair all the time." I lifted my hand backwards in acknowledgement and continued walking.

As is often true in public nursing homes, an air of poverty and smelly neglect clung to the walls—an air not dispelled by the highly burnished linoleum floors. Despite a surface polish, these were the corridors of yesterday's dreams, echoing with the faint voices of men and women whose days were mostly done. Family members and friends living far away were often both guilty and relieved when they couldn't visit regularly; those living nearby struggled with the burdens of proximity. And everyone—residents, staff, and visitors—knew a truth no one voiced: these endless lonely hallways couldn't take a real shine. It was not in their nature.

The nurse was correct, Mr. B. wasn't in his room. That wasn't surprising—the room embodied the essence of drear and was a marriage of dingy cast-offs: two side chairs with cracked gray vinyl seats, two food trays on wheels, two single beds, two scarred and mismatched bureaus, bare walls, overhead lighting. Standing there, I wondered how I'd be able to pull off my mission. I'd been asked to come to the nursing home to see Mr. B.'s wife because they were one-time members of an Episcopal church in northern Virginia where I now worked, and it seemed she was ill. When I found her, however, it turned out she wanted a pastoral visit for her husband.

"He needs company far more than I do, dear," she said. Her loud sigh suggested that she wasn't too keen on providing that company. "Though we don't live together anymore, I do see him. I try to lift his spirits, but nothing seems to help. And his roommate is bad tempered, probably because Mr. B. can't speak. It's so much work to communicate with him—even having him write things down is hard because of his terrible arthritis. I would so appreciate it if you would visit him, say a prayer with him." I agreed to do this, no longer perplexed about why Mr. B.

now lived with a roommate.

Without a clue where he might be, I set off from his room to find him. It didn't take long. Coming around a corner I spied a man I guessed was he, sitting in an alcove, slumped in a wheelchair, his back to me, staring out a large plate glass window at the rain.

I came around his side slowly. "Are you Mr. B.?" I asked tentatively, as he swiveled his head toward me. He nodded without smiling. I stuck out my hand and said, "My name is Mary. I'm a pastoral associate from the church. I wanted to come pay a call on you." He shook my hand absently, took in my clerical collar, looked frankly up and down the rest of me, and turned back to the rain. In a side pocket on the wheelchair there was a spiral notebook and, tied to the chair's arm, a pencil dangling on a string.

I sat down on a narrow window seat a couple of feet away from him. He was a study in dishevelment: baggy, worn-out pants cinched by a wide belt; a graying white shirt with a frayed collar; threadbare sweater; badly scuffed shoes, no socks. Though he was shaved, whoever did the job had missed some places, so he had a number of hairy white tufts on his cheeks and neck. His eighty-year-old face was a long, heavily creased slab...once-upon-a-time handsome. His dark brown eyes were clouded by cataracts and, I guessed, deep-dyed loneliness.

After sitting in silence for a minute, I said, "Mr. B., I know you had a stroke many years back and that you can't speak." He looked at me dubiously and then thrust gnarled parallel index fingers toward me in a parody of numbers. "Eleven years ago?" I asked. He nodded. "Eleven years is a long time not to be able to talk," I said. "And I'm guessing that it has also been a long frustrating time?" He nodded again. His head bobbed up and down so vehemently that a string of spittle got loose and threaded across his chin. He drew his sleeve over his mouth and then dropped both knobby hands in his lap, as though any attempt to communicate was too wearying.

"Listen," I said, after a pause, as I leaned forward, "It's hard that you can't talk. I mean it's hard for you, and it's also hard for others, including me. I'll promise you something up front, though. I'd like to come and see you for pastoral visits and I won't give up on you just because you can't talk." He looked me full in my face and rolled his eyes.

"I mean it," I said, and then, on a hunch, plunged in where I hadn't yet been invited. "Have people given up on you in the past because you can't speak?" He averted his eyes, shrugging off an answer that was part yes, part maybe, mostly what-the-hell-is-it-to-you. Already, I liked this man plenty.

"Well, I won't do that," I said. "And I'll make you a second promise. I'm not going to talk your ears off. I assume you talk using that notepad that's hanging off your chair, but it may wear you out. We can go for walks, we might listen to music, but we don't have to talk. And I'll bring you Communion if you want." He looked into my face again, no eye rolls this time. Instead, a tentative smile. "You like that idea, Communion?" I asked. The smile deepened into a grin and stuck. "Well, you'll have it, then, by early next week. No, let's say for sure: next Tuesday afternoon around 2:00." He reached for his notebook and wrote *is that a promise?* It was my turn to grin.

"And now how about taking a ride down to the cafeteria for a cup of coffee?" I said. He hesitated for a fraction and then unlocked the wheelchair brake. "I'd offer to push the chair," I said, "but I suspect you'd rather do that yourself." He answered by bringing his hands down firmly on the wheels and leaned into a large burst of upper body strength. I gathered my bag and raincoat and, walking fast to keep up with him, we were off.

The following Tuesday afternoon was warm, the air light with the fragrance of azaleas and flowering dogwood—the lovely lady Virginia, a-bloom in late April. Shortly before 2:00, with my Communion kit under my arm, I followed an outside walkway I guessed ran in front of the window where I'd found Mr. B. the week before. And there he was again, his wheelchair in the same spot. I waved, he waved back and my heart contracted, realizing he'd been waiting for me.

What if I disappointed him? Not in failing to show up; after all, here I was. First promise kept. But what about the promise not to talk his ears off? I knew well that anxiety could steal my consciousness, sometimes making me talk too much. I redoubled my determination not to let that happen. Granted, a pastoral visit with someone who can't speak is a daunting prospect. And I'd never done it before. I also knew, though, that if I stayed grounded in my truest self, not giving way to anxiety, deep would eventually speak to deep. Whether in words or silence didn't matter. I opened the door and stepped inside the hall, darker than usual after the sunlight.

Mr. B. knew where I would enter the building and came wheeling to meet me. I was touched to see that he looked more spruced up today. Besides wearing a better shirt, he had socks on, and his cheeks weren't sporting any white patches. He rolled to a stop in front of me, held out his hand. I grasped it firmly, noting how strong his grip felt this time. I was to learn a lot about his hands in subsequent weeks, gradually realizing how much talking he did with them.

"I'm very glad to see you again, Mr. B.," I said. He smiled at me for real, which I took to mean he felt the same. "Would you like to go for a walk, or rather, a ride for you and a walk for me? It's lovely outside." He grabbed his notebook. *I'll walk, lean on your arm*, he wrote. "Fine," I said, chagrinned that I hadn't asked whether he always needed the wheelchair. I then said, "Let's first put this Communion kit in your room for when we come back?" With a silent whoop, he led the way.

In Mr. B.'s room we had a brief fumbling pause. He locked the wheelchair brake, with my kit in its seat, and then he held up his notebook, looking questioningly at me. "Sure," I said. "Bring it. I can carry it in my pocketbook." A shadow of indecision fell across his face. "Are you worried I'll forget to give it back?" He nodded. "I won't." He cocked his head as a smile curled around his question. "Yes," I said, "another promise." He handed over the notebook and I offered him my arm.

Once we were outside, I heard an enormous sigh escape—not from Mr. B.'s lips so much as from his spirit. He drank in the sun and the cobalt sky, as though slaking a profound thirst, and radiated the relief of a prisoner sprung from his chains. As he piloted us, arm in arm, slowly down the sidewalk running next to the nursing home, I could feel his body relaxing, his step surprisingly sure for a man who spent much of his time in a wheelchair.

Ambling along, I worked to quell an urge to chat and fill the void created by his silence. And then I stole a look at the side of his face: it shone with happiness simply to be here, to be alive, in a moment I realized was anything but "mute." I understood now that what he probably craved was silence *not* filled with chat. Real talk, maybe, but not small talk, not someone chittering into his ears. As contentment streamed from him, I realized that the soft Virginia afternoon, someone to walk with, a willing arm to lean on...it was enough. Reaching over with my free hand and patting his arm linked in mine, I was flooded with— and silenced by—my own gratitude at being here with him.

We walked for a short distance. Mr. B. paused occasionally to sniff the white fringe trees, the dark magenta and lavender lilacs, each time flashing me a look of delight. At one point, in front of a plush bed of bright pink viburnum, he closed his eyes and took in a large draft of their sweetness, seeming to store the perfume for future use once he was inside again. It was true: everything outside smelled fresh and clean and infused the memory of the Lysol-swabbed hallways with extra melancholy.

After we had walked for some minutes, I spied a bench and asked Mr. B. if he wanted to rest for a bit. He did. He had already stopped a couple of times and pointed with interest at people who looked to me like volunteer gardeners, and I'd said as much to him. There were two women close by this bench, on their hands and knees, so it seemed like a good place to sit down and inquire.

"Excuse me for interrupting you," I said. "Are you volunteering, doing this gardening?"

"Oh, yes," said one of the women, her face streaked with sweat, "we come here every week, three seasons of the year." The other woman laughed. "We're members of a small, dedicated, and very happy army."

"What a great gift," I said. "I wondered, because no public nursing home is likely to be able to afford this kind of landscaping."

"That's right," one of them said. "We're part of a volunteer group in town that raises money for plantings at all sorts of locations, and then we tend what has been planted."

Mr. B. pointed toward my pocketbook, gesturing that he wanted to write something. I handed him his notebook and a pen and in shaky script he scratched out, *Thank you so much. These gardens make me feel alive.* When I showed his words to the women, they were visibly moved.

"How nice of you to say that," one remarked to him. We exchanged a few more words and then the women went on to another spot to work. Mr. B. picked up the notebook and pen again.

I used to have a garden, he wrote.

"You mean where you lived, here in town?" He nodded.

"And that was something you got a lot of pleasure from?" I asked.

Yes, not much money, but rich in flowers.

"Which may partly explain why you seem rich in spirit," I said.

Do I?

"To me, yes."

I almost always could find God in the garden.

"No wonder you were keen to come out here this afternoon," I said.

Yes, he wrote, jerking his head back toward the nursing home, *it's hard for me to find God inside that place.*

"I hear you," I said. "Maybe celebrating Communion in your room will change that a little. I'm sort of reluctant, myself, to go inside again. If we want to have Communion, though, I guess we need to start back." Before we stood up I asked him something I had wanted to know for a while: what he had done for work.

Machinist, he wrote. *Over 60 years.* He looked up from the notebook, gave me a wistful smile, and then added, *I liked machining.*

"What did you like about it?" I asked.

Took brains and strength. And patience. Like gardening.

He handed me the notebook, then took it back. *Thank you for asking me about my work. It has been so long since I felt useful.*

"You're welcome," I said, stifling another urge to gabble on—especially after this last admission. There were obviously layers of strong feeling under what he wrote, layers I wanted to make room for, to explore with him. But so far, conversation with Mr. B. had proved to be full of thorny ironies. I noticed he winced in the task of writing, presumably because of his arthritis. I didn't like being the prompt for his pain. At the same time, loneliness came off him like a strong scent and it bothered me not to respond to him more fulsomely. If I overplayed the difficulty of communicating with him, though, it would just fan his fears that I would become impatient and, like other people before me, desert him in frustration.

Feeling divided by all this, I stood up, held out my elbow, and said, "Thanks for telling me a bit about yourself. I like that...I like knowing you a little better." He settled his arm again in mine. Sporting another crooked grin, he seemed satisfied with my words. Many subjects, like his sense of uselessness and the loneliness of his days, might have to go unaddressed because there was no good way to discuss complex things. As the poet Stanley Kunitz once put it, perhaps the only way for me to "live in the layers" with Mr. B would be through willingness to live largely in layers of silence, learning to relax into its strange eloquence. As I embraced that concept, wondering about it, we walked back: slowly, quietly, still mutually pleased by the loveliness of the day—a pleasure heard mostly in the murmur of pressure between Mr. B's right arm hooked into my left.

When we arrived back in his room, I felt relieved that his roommate was elsewhere. I didn't want company while I navigated through this celebration of Holy Communion, and I particularly didn't want to have to deal with a roommate's bad temper—as reported by Mr. B's wife.

Mr. B. now seemed relaxed. Handing me my Communion kit, he lowered himself into his wheelchair with a satisfied sigh, as if he'd just polished off a great meal. I said as much to him, laughing, and he made a motion of wanting to write in his notebook. I retrieved it from my pocketbook, saying, "Promise kept," and began to convert one of the rolling food trays into a makeshift altar.

I laid out a small white cloth from my kit and then placed the kit's miniature sterling silver contents on the cloth: a tiny chalice and plate for the already-consecrated wine and wafers I'd brought, the round container that held the wafers, two small silver-topped glass cruets—one filled with water, the other with wine. I also retrieved my abbreviated version of the Book of Common Prayer, reassured to have it close by.

Mr. B., meanwhile, had wheeled himself over to the food tray. He creased his notebook open, shyly venturing the new page toward me, where I read:

> *Thank you, God, for finding me today in the sun.*
> *Thank you for everything green. Thank you for*
> *bringing me a companion. Henry*

His gratitude charged the air with the intimacy of pain revealed; in return, I looked squarely at him.

"May I call you Henry?" I asked. He nodded. He then leaned forward in his wheelchair and motioned for me to give him my hands, which he took into both of his. And then slowly, gently, but firmly, kneading my hands all over, this old machinist, this once-upon-a-time gardener, told me more about himself than a hundred conversations might have done.

After letting these moments spend themselves, I suggested to him that we ought to move forward and asked if it was okay to incorporate his words of thanksgiving into the Communion service.

"What you've written amounts to a prayer, after all," I said. He assented, indicating he was pleased. I decided, then, to abandon the Prayer Book and simply went forward improvising—weaving together his written words and my spoken ones, with silences and phrases from the Communion service that I knew by heart and believed would be most familiar and comforting to him. He kept his hand on my arm the whole time, his eyes mostly closed, sunk into a stillness and emotional presence far below words. We didn't hurry. When I eventually began the

Lord's Prayer, he moved his lips to its familiar old ca-
dence, his fingers pressing into my arm a message as indel-
ible as if he'd actually spoken it: thank you for finding me,
thank you for caring for me, thank you for walking me
back into my own way of experiencing the love of God.

Undone, once again, by the intimacy of the moment,
and by his faithful surrender to it, I panicked slightly
about bringing the service to a close. There was no need
for concern; the rhythms of it all were running like a mem-
orized poem through his blood. Without any prompting,
he simply held out his hands to receive the wafer, and offered his mouth to take the thimbleful of wine I lifted to
him. As he smiled at me, I marveled at how rarely God
gets such an eager guest at the feast.

And so we went on, for many months; me coming every
couple of weeks and he at the window each time to greet
me—in season and out. Occasionally I had to contend
briefly with the roommate, but he made himself scarce
when I showed up. I suspected he was unnerved by the
appearance of a clerical collar in his room, which seemed a
good use of it.

As for Henry and me, we continued our round of
simple graces: walking inside and out, going to the cafeteria, sharing thoughts, sometimes sitting and holding hands
in silence, celebrating Communion. I often brought along a
small bunch of flowers from the churchyard to place on
the rolling altar; I never again brought the Book of Com-

mon Prayer.

We also continued over those months to deepen the relationship, to learn much more about one another. I was wrong in my early assumption that there was no way to explore complexities in Henry's life—and in my own—simply because talk was impossible and he couldn't write without pain. When he wanted to say something, he wrote through the pain.

I came to understand a difference between talking and speaking. While talk eluded Henry, he spoke in his writing with a deep ease of spirit. It turned out that he was not bitter about the inability to talk; he was just frustrated—hardly the same thing. Whatever sadness he harbored settled mostly on the distant relationship with his wife, and on his son, an only child he'd lost to cancer years earlier. In telling of his hardscrabble childhood, there wasn't a trace of regret. Instead, his heart seemed full of appreciation for parents who had loved him well, despite their meager means.

And when it was my turn, because for sure he wanted to know about me, he had the two singular qualities of a good listener: curiosity and all-the-time-in-the-world. In hearing a bit about my own checkered past, complete with a divorce history very odd for a clergywoman, he registered no censoring, only affectionate regard. My intuition proved true. He did want real talk, I just needed to be willing to move along the path slowly. I occasionally had to take a large tuck in my impatience, my tendency to hurry, because time spent with Henry was time in the slow lane.

But the price was small and the rewards were great.

Perhaps best of all, I came to a redoubled understanding about the glories of silence. It was I who had been anxious about this, while silence was mostly where Henry lived, day after day. It was I who lived in the noisy, busy, jazzed up world; in comparison, his existence was almost monastic in its companionship with silence. He was just looking for someone willing to join him there—in silence and in sound.

All this continued until a phone call I had dreaded came into the church office one morning. It was the nursing home, calling to say that Henry had suffered another stroke. He was in the hospital and wasn't expected to live long. I was pulling my coat on before they said his wife had asked whether I planned to go and administer Last Rites; I was soon sprinting through the rain to my car.

Again, long shiny corridors paved the way to his room, but these halls rang with the sounds and smells of modern medicine, the whir of technology. It wasn't necessarily cheerier than the nursing home—just tricked out to make it feel like a place of life rather than death. And so it often was, until it wasn't.

I rounded past a nursing station with some nurses I knew from other patient visits; when I called out Henry's name they pointed me toward his room with sympathetic encouragement, aware of why I had come. I drank the silent support like a bracing cup of tea.

And then, there he was. In a single room, blanketed in stillness, window curtains pulled. Still alive. Wanting not to rend the quiet, I gingerly lifted a chair to the side of the bed, sat down, and slipped my hand into his. Nothing.

"Henry, try to squeeze my hand if you know it's me, Mary."

Faint pressure from his hand into mine.

"Good."

I waited for what felt like forever, watching his chest rise and fall. Hearing only the drum of my own blood in my ears, I said, "I think you understand that you are dying, Henry. Please squeeze my hand again if you do."

Another squeeze, this one a bit firmer.

"Okay, my dear old friend, I've come to keep you company, to say some prayers, and to anoint your spirit for the journey. Squeeze my hand again if you like that plan."

He squeezed a third time, the strongest yet. I said, "I'm going to go find more of these ice chips, get a clean cloth for your mouth, and ask the nurses to ask the aides to leave us in peace." He smiled and nodded, his eyes closed.

When I returned after a few minutes, his head had lolled to one side, his mouth was slack, his features were changed in the way that only death can change them...he was on his way.

I started to cry. I sat back down in the chair and took his hand again, listening to the silence death leaves behind. I yearned, of course, to shake him awake—believing, like children everywhere, that death had to be a bad joke, that it wasn't for real. But here it was: the still body, the flown spirit, the company no longer there to be kept.

And then I saw what was probably the truth. Like many another dying person, Henry had taken his moment to go when he was left alone. I should have guessed it. This bright, sensitive, non-talking man with a deeply playful sense of humor had given himself the last word. One hesitates, always, to place so certain a conclusion on a death that happens this way. But in light of Henry's singular loneliness and the balm he and I had applied to that wound, it was a reasonable hunch.

As I made the sign of the cross on his forehead with the oil I'd brought, words from the old version of the 23rd Psalm, which I knew Henry knew by heart, streamed out of my mouth like a banner, a holy pennant marking the end of one journey and the start of the next. As I held the side of his face, I spoke the ancient words for both our sakes into the silence that felt suddenly bracing:

> *Yea, though I walk through the*
> *valley of the shadow of death,*
> *I shall fear no evil;*
> *for thou art with me;*
> *thy rod and thy staff, they comfort me...*

I kissed him on the forehead. *The Lord bless and keep you, Henry, now and evermore.* Touching his hand, I then gathered my things and took a last look at him before leaving the room. As I shut the door behind me, I thought how it would have amused Henry—as it did me—to imagine the blast from a golden trumpet...and ah, bright wings!

The Widow's Mite

As a kid, I was afraid of Ida. And small wonder: at six feet tall and climbing, with big hands and a severe face, she was every inch a forbidding Yankee woman. She lived in a shuttered, rundown farmhouse with a herd of mangy cats on the Maine island my family went to every summer. Childhood friends who had experienced her as a teacher at the island grammar school only amplified my anxieties. When we quickened our pace passing her dark house on a summer night and they whispered, *Thank your lucky stars she didn't teach you math*, I thanked my stars heartily— being an accomplished math numbskull.

Among grown-ups, Ida was an object of tongue-clucking from islanders and summer residents alike, in part because of her derelict house, but mostly because of her eccentricities. She was an isolated figure upon whom others could easily hang a bit of self-righteousness. Once upon a time Ida had subsisted on her meager teacher's salary; long before she died, though, what she lived on was a mystery. We took contrary pleasure in rumors of her eating canned cat food to hold body and soul together and gleefully speculated on what she might be doing in the solitary reaches of her house. This gossip made my father chide the rest of us for being so uncharitable. But I lapped up the chatter as long as Ida's person remained at arm's length.

When I was about ten years old my image of Ida shifted slightly one summer morning. My best friend Helen, an island girl, and I were slipping down the lane beside Ida's house on our way to the shore. We pretended not to notice that she was sitting in the wide doorway of her barn until she cut through our nonchalance by calling us to come over and visit with her for a minute. Helen and I hesitated, but then joined hands and walked across the yard to the barn. Just inside, on an old wooden rocker, Ida sat in a patch of sunlight.

I soon had to admit to myself that it was pleasant to stand in the door while she went on braiding a rug and the sun streamed into the barn's musty interior. As I listened to the creak of her chair, smelled the warm floor boards, watched her big hands deftly form braids out of cloth long since faded to soft reds and blues, she making small talk to our tied tongues, I wondered whether she was quite as fierce as her reputation. She just looked poor, and worn out. I didn't know then that she was a first-rate rug maker. I would have stayed longer to watch, but Helen was not especially mesmerized—her own grandmother braided rugs by the dozen—and she didn't much care for this close-up of Ida. After a few minutes, Helen pulled us away. She said we were going swimming at the back shore, a plan which brought a gap-toothed, mischievous smile from Ida. We were soon giggling on down the lane toward the beach as we shivered at our proximity to a childhood mystery figure, now somewhat reduced in size.

Over the succeeding years I saw Ida rarely—maybe as she was pinning a bed sheet onto a clothesline in her back yard, or riding on the boat over to the mainland. She would acknowledge me or someone else in my family by name, knowing well who we all were, but there was an invisible divide, a distance, between Ida and most others. That distance was especially clear to a family like mine, who were summer people.

It was as summer people going home that my mother and two younger sisters and I went to the island in the heart of winter to bury my father, now more than forty years ago. The island was bleak in the February cold: closed, spare, and quiet. Not much moved except the smoke from chimneys and an occasional car making its cautious way down roads packed hard with snow. Even the pine trees seemed lonesome; standing black against the sky like widows staring out to sea. For a family used to the bright blue of summer and the freedom of running through long grass, the snowbound winter felt confining and harsh—a good match for the small rough opening at the island cemetery where we would soon place my father's ashes.

In our house during that week, there was little to be

glad about. We were grateful for simple things—a fire in the Franklin stove, letters that poured in, the sympathy of neighbors, the comfort of one another as we tried to eat, to sleep, to read, and mostly failed at everything.

One evening as the four of us gathered in the living room around the fire, in a doleful scene reminiscent of *Little Women*, one of my sisters said she heard a rap at the kitchen door. It was late and snowing hard. As I went to check on this knock I felt impatient and anxious, not wanting to respond to another intrusion on my own grief. In addition, when I got to the kitchen I could see there was no one at the door. Muttering that my sister had heard a ghost, I yanked the door open and started to snap the outside porch light off. I hesitated. Down at the bottom of the back steps, in the shadows at the edge of the circle of porch light, there was a figure.

In an icy slant of snow, Ida stood with one arm clutching her threadbare coat around her middle, the other holding out a large aluminum pan. "I thought you folks might like to have this chocolate cake," she said. "It isn't much, but it's what I've got." She turned to go. Recovering my wits, I stammered out a thank you and then called to her. "Ida, won't you come in and sit by the fire?" She turned again, bent toward me and said in a voice barely audible, "No, I won't do that. But I will remember your father...he was always so kind to me."

And then she was gone, her eighty-year old frame \ by the dark and the howl of wind as she lum- up the road: no hat, no gloves, no scarf. Nothing but her gracious offering left behind with me, rooted on the steps in the swirling snow, my grateful heart cracking.

Abide with Me

It was a short walk from the lobby of the funeral home to the room where my mother's body was being kept, and it took all my fifty-nine years to make the trip.

During the previous three days and nights, my two younger sisters and I and a very pregnant niece had stood watch, in the assisted living facility, over my mother's dying—monitoring a train of labored breaths which finally stopped, dead, just after midnight. Stretched out like cordwood on the floor of my mother's room, sleeping fitfully, my sisters and I leapt up in one scrambled motion at the sound of sudden silence, certain before we checked: she was gone.

In the hours leading up to her death, we hadn't discussed what we would do when it happened. Now, instinct took over. In between serial bouts of tears, we attended to her. We removed her nightgown, washing her all over as perhaps only daughters can do for mothers, and put on her dress, sweater, socks, shoes. We registered the irony of this body care, she having done it for us as children, and we were awed by how young her face now seemed, with its end-of-life stress erased. We didn't hurry to inform the staff that she had died; we knew once we did they would call the funeral home to come take her away, and we wanted to delay the moment.

By early morning, with that moment at hand, a collective tremble took us over. Two men wheeled in a gurney carrying an open body bag. They were kind, but hearing the zipper close her in was not. The men quickly left with her—well aware that, like a bandage needing to be ripped off fast, there was no gain in hesitation. As the finality of it coursed through us, we collapsed into a messy heap, each fighting with our own sorrows. No matter how grown up we were, the loss of our second parent had orphaned us: children forever, at any age.

Later on the morning my mother died, carrying my own handful of sorrows, I ventured into the small, chilly anteroom where they were holding her body. My sisters had opted not to see her there, a choice I well understood and could not make for myself. Of the three of us, my relationship with my mother had in many ways been the most fraught. I knew that I needed to spend some time with her, to begin to splice together strands of my regret, forgiveness, and gratitude. At the end of her life, she and I hadn't spoken of our early sharp edges; her severe dementia precluded it. And we hadn't spoken of them much any time *before* the end—God forbid we should be so direct. But like a curtain, trouble had hung between us for years. And now I meant to draw back that curtain, for both our sakes. No matter where *she* was, I was still here.

Sitting down next to her, I initially felt fearful. It wasn't the fact of her being dead. As a clergywoman, I had seen enough corpses—in hospital beds, nursing facilities, funeral homes—to feel comfortable with their cold, alabaster stillness. *But this was my mother.* These were the arms that had once pushed my pram through Gramercy Park, the lap I'd jumped into, the face that had enchanted me with its smile or scared me when it went tight and dark. Hers could never be, in other words, simply another body to me. It could only be *her* body, and at first, I feared that thought.

I touched her forehead. I was tentative, then more resolute, and finally I stroked her whole face. For an instant, I thought she might smile or murmur with pleasure. But the dead are so indisputably dead. Eyelids will not flutter; lips will not part; stomachs won't rise and fall, no matter how hard we stare. I pulled my chair closer. I felt my fear start to ebb. The hands on some old, faraway mantle clock inched forward, flooding me with memory.

As a person and as a mother, she was a kaleidoscope of shifting fragments.

Some things I knew about her from stories and photographs. The day she asked to be dropped off from a sailboat, by friends, onto a bell buoy clanging in the rolling ocean. The time she ran naked from the waist up in public, on a dare. The afternoon she steered her sailboat into the teeth of a howling wind, exulting like Ahab.

And I knew much more from my own experience of her. How righteously she could lunge for a well-worn Webster's to prove yet another pronunciation; her thunder against my protest at sixteen that I had *not*, as she furiously insisted, slept with a boyfriend; her endless crankiness about my father's mother, who lived with us for years, until she finally shoehorned her into a nursing home.

To be sure, without her guidance I would never have taken *Middlemarch* to my bosom as a favorite book, or learned to cook flawless baked custard, or understood how to create a cozy home with little money. I wouldn't have known from an early age how to lay a successful fire in a woodstove, make a lusciously comfortable bed, divine the tricks for becoming a champion speller. She was strong-minded, ardent, and ferociously competent. Since those qualities cut sharply in two directions, though, she became for me a daunting strenuous blessing: glory if I made the grade, shame if I did not, with either outcome likely to produce emotional vertigo in me.

Sitting next to her, taking in the oddity of her deadness, I recalled an experience she had thought would be amusing at the time, but that typified how disorienting her behavior could be to me, even as a young child. In preparation for a Halloween party when I was in first grade, she spent countless hours making a costume designed to transform me into The Phantom of the Opera. She assembled a white bib shirt, black tails and white tie, a long red cape and top hat, and then completed the effect with a rubber mask that turned me into a miniature Lon Chaney. This conversion struck her as wildly successful and made her roar with laughter.

Unfortunately, however, when I saw myself in a mirror on Halloween morning, I became hysterical at my hideousness, especially at the mask, and bawled without letup. My mother was furious. But she brooked no debate. I was going to wear the costume to school, and I was going to walk the couple of blocks there as usual. Furthermore, she assured me, as she steered me down the front steps of the house and waved me off, all the kids at the Halloween party were going to nominate me for Most Creative Costume...

I never got to school. At least I never made it inside, or to the party. Instead, I spent the morning traipsing back and forth along the chain link fence that surrounded the schoolyard. My red cape dragged on the dirty sidewalk; the hated mask hung askew. It wasn't until the bell rang and kids poured outside for recess that another child spied me by the fence and told the teacher, who came to investigate.

Of course, I've long known this story is funny. Pathetic, but funny in the way many childhood stories are, with a parent captured by a project far beyond a child's capacity to appreciate, and a child awash in mortification never intended. My mother was soon chagrinned, I got past my tears...and yet as I sat there now, caressing her cold arm, that painful morning was quick to flash through me again.

Why was the memory so durable? I think because, even back then, I knew my mother's exasperation was stronger than her chagrin, and this knowledge acted as a kind of memory fixative. The struggle inside her between anger at me and ruefulness *over* her anger was never-ending. It wove a web of misunderstanding that continued to ensnare us for years to come.

In me there was an echoing struggle, just as strong, between defiance and concession. I so longed for her approval and I was a master at behavior that caused me to forfeit it—over and over again. I don't just mean small or silly misbehaviors, but large ones, like doing poorly in high school and then equally poorly in an initial attempt at college; persisting against her wishes in a marriage that I couldn't admit was a terrible mistake; pursuing a series of jobs that didn't match either my abilities or my upbringing.

The strain between us was the background music in many disparate circumstances. It was there on the morning she and my father stood far below me on a pier, all of us waving as I hung over the railing of a decrepit ocean liner pulling out of New York Harbor. At barely nineteen, a freshly minted college failure, I was off to spend a year working on a kibbutz in Israel. This was a gap-year idea back in the early 1960's, popular among some of my family's Jewish friends, and one didn't need to be Jewish to pursue it. My mother in particular had latched onto the plan with great enthusiasm; I yielded to it because I didn't have a better idea.

What I most remember about that day, though, is not the lunacy of setting out alone while I was barely dry behind the ears. Nor was it the travel to a country a world away that had recently emerged from a war. Instead, my memory is haunted by the conviction I had back then that my mother was, deep down, glad to see me go. I believed what she said, that she was scared for my safety. But I also believed what she didn't say: that if my errant self went elsewhere for a good long time it would be fine by her.

These many years later, I could roll my eyes in genuine amusement at why she might have dispatched me with great relief. But on that day, I remember feeling a pervasive sadness, a homesickness I was too young to name. It wasn't just because I was leaving. The feeling crystalized in the flutter of an orange silk neck scarf she wore—the liveliness of it symbolizing what I had yearned for in a relationship with her, but only fleetingly experienced. And now, sitting beside her body, I could still feel the sadness I experienced back then, watching that scarf get smaller and smaller while we glided out of the harbor, until it finally became just a bright orange dot and then disappeared from sight when the ship rounded a bend in the Hudson River.

My mother could not have known on that long ago day— as I did not—that my leaving would kick-start some comprehension of the strengths I'd inherited from her. Almost as soon as the ship was ocean bound, it hit me like a one-two punch: I was plunging solo into the unknown, and had no clue how I'd manage. I was confident that once I got to the kibbutz, older adults would be there to offer some guidance and protection; even so, it suddenly struck me I was going to sink or swim by my own wits. I wasn't yet aware that my mother would turn up, often, at the edge of my consciousness.

For example, a few weeks after I arrived at the kib-butz, I was engaged in some demanding chore in the huge communal kitchen, surprised at my own reserves of ener-gy and zeal. For years I'd ingested the not-so-subtle infer-ence from my mother that I was lazy and not particularly capable, assuming it was the truth. It wasn't until a couple of kibbutz women sweating alongside me asked, "Where did you learn to work so hard," that I heard myself mutter-ing, "Where indeed..." and then, laughing for real, replied with the one true answer, "from my mother!"

When I was younger, I had *despised* what sounded like moralizing exhortations to lace into a job, not stop until it was done, and to be sure I did it well. But once I was mak-ing my own way, in an alien country nine thousand miles from home, working from sunup to sundown at tasks that stretched every physical and emotional muscle, it was my mother's voice that whispered "Atta girl" in my ear. Could I, at nineteen, hear the encouragement in it? Not really—I was too primed to hear criticism. Was I ever able, in sub-sequent years, to talk with her about the complicated debt

I owed her? No—we were unlikely to invite such vulnerability. But her whisper, however faint, that I experienced over the months I lived on the kibbutz was the start of figuring out some new things about who she was and what she meant to me.

I didn't understand until much later in life that the tasks themselves were never the point. Oh, they have to get done, and credibly, and she was right: I *did* need to quit carping and help her finish varnishing the brightwork on her sailboat, to stop the adolescent whining and just hang up the damn laundry, to stow my boggy complaints about writing a term paper for school and simply write it. But it took a long time to figure out that my mother's fundamental desire, which I mistook for years as synonymous with the tasks, was to create a certain appetite in me, a zestful passion for living. She knew that when we lack such passion, all is lost. And she knew it because she herself had it. She didn't give a fig about hanging out the wash on a glorious summer day—she wanted to go sailing!

Many contests of wills, however, were required for me to reach that understanding. Much of the time, during my growing up and way beyond, she brought control to the contest and I brought argument.

During my mid-teens, for instance, she insisted I wear hand-me-down clothes from the daughter of a friend of hers. The girl was supremely popular at our school, so this meant I would be going to school in clothes just shed by a star. From the current perspective of advanced age, complaining about this smacks of brathood. But at fourteen:

mortification! Although my mother claimed that there wasn't enough money for new clothes, I knew this was mostly malarkey. I refused to wear the clothes, she refused to buy me others, insisting the hand-me-downs were perfectly good...and of course I eventually wore them, brathood in full flower.

Then there was the day, years later, when we got embroiled in yet another fashion quarrel—this time about what I ought to wear for my second wedding. One would think that, at thirty years old, such a decision would fall squarely to me. But driving around and around Portland, arguing about the appropriate outfit, we repeatedly circled the real point: that I couldn't wrest the reins of my own life from her grip. No wonder the wedding outfit was a hit and the marriage a dismal failure.

A number of years later, as I continued to lick my wounds from the divorce, my mother and I finally had a long-overdue donneybrook. It happened on a stormy February night when she drove to my apartment in Portland, where I'd been living alone, to share a dinner with me and spend the night. I had knocked myself out making the meal and had cleaned my apartment to a fare-thee-well.

About half way into the evening, I realized I was getting far too much criticism from her. I collated my courage and told her if her critical tongue was the best she could offer she was welcome to sleep elsewhere. With my heart beating in my throat like a trapped bird, I ended up ushering her out to her car half-buried in snow. Minutes later, when I called my youngest sister in Boston to say I was sure she would have our mother on her doorstep before the night was over, I felt both frightened and gleeful: anxious about the stormy weather, inside and out, and relieved at having stood up to her. Over the next few days every fiber of my being taunted me to cave in, but for once I did nothing.

And then a letter came from her, full of abject apology, real remorse, and desire for forgiveness. Without exaggeration, it was a moment of profound conversion in our relationship. Things were not smooth from then on, but we moved onto new ground. And although I continued to struggle with which of us had hold of the reins, over time I was able to gain far more balance in my behavior and my feelings. I could summon vivid memories of prior good times with her. When I joined these with recent good experiences, the harsher, older memories—though not erased—were much less insistent.

And now, in these last moments spent with her body, I found gratitude easy to come by. The funeral parlor did not help in this—smelling as it did of cheap furniture oil and strangers' grief. The room also housed a forest of potted palms, all of which were stiff and cheerless, like the bodies temporarily placed there. But in part because of the intense gloominess of it—which my mother would have chortled at—I could recall with thanks how often she and I had sat together in her snug living room, next to a crackling fire in the Franklin stove. We once whiled away an entire evening there reading sections of *The Country of the Pointed Firs* aloud to each other, moved to tears by the same passages. I saw again the many peaceful cups of tea, the high-spirited Scrabble games, with me making plenty of my own self-righteous beelines to Webster's. And I remembered a golden night when I was a freshman in high school. She and my father were taking me to Sardi's in New York, to an opening night party to celebrate a new Broadway musical for which my father was the press agent. For days on end, I'd been weak with excitement about this event. My mother understood exactly why, and the costume she helped me assemble *that* time thrilled me to the bottom of my teenaged toes.

Not long after she wrote the note of apology to me in my mid-thirties, fresh insights about her started to form. For one thing, I saw that, like many other women of her time—and plenty of women before and since—my mother had great difficulty finding a large enough life. As a bright college graduate of the late 1930's, sporting a strong stripe of rebelliousness and derring-do, part of her yearned for adventures beyond what hearth and home could provide. But she fell in love and married. And when World War II took my father off to Europe, she didn't yearn for anything larger than his return, intact—which, rejoicing, she got.

Secondly, although I knew she loved my father dearly, and my sisters and me as well, and did enjoy our life as a family, chafing against the fetters of domesticity made her volatile a lot of the time. Once the lens I had for her widened, I gradually realized that her volatility sprang from multiple sources—of which I was only one. When that understanding took root, I stopped feeling constantly at fault and could forgive her much more easily.

Thirdly, over time I gained an empathetic appreciation of an event I was aware of but she had always refused to discuss—that before she had me, she'd given birth to still-born, full-term twin boys. Her unwillingness to speak of this loss only amplified it. As I approached forty years old, a troubling awareness of my own began to dawn: a loudly ticking biological clock and a tattered marital history might well mean I wouldn't have my own children. Mentioning this hunch to my mother, the look of pained comprehension she shot me made clear what she knew: when the promise of longed-for children dies, a deep and singular grief is born. We never talked about either her past grief or mine to come, but I've carried her wordless commiseration for long years now and will remain eternally grateful for it.

At the end, that gratitude was the point. While I could still touch her, before the inexorable hand of time turned her into ashes, I needed to speak my hard-won thanks out loud. To tell her that what I'd received from her, finally, far outweighed whatever I hadn't. Many of her strengths had long since become my own. And I needed to say that although it was true the price on our affections had once been uncommonly high, everything was now okay, having been gathered in by the long arm of forgiveness.

We buried my mother at the island cemetery on an overcast March day—in a stiff breeze that would have pleased her sailor's heart. Beforehand, in the church, I had been tapped to give a eulogy. I had a notion I might sing at the end of my remarks, while I was still up in the pulpit, but I wasn't sure I'd be able to make it through *any* music. When I came to the end, though, I just decided to go for it: for her sake, for my own. After all, as I've said, I wasn't sure where she was, but I was still here.

I sang a fragment of an old Joe Hill song that both my parents loved, called "The Rebel Girl." For a host of reasons this song was my mother personified; it was no accident that Rebel Girl was the name of her last boat:

> *There are women of many descriptions...*
> *In this queer world as everyone knows*
> *Some are living in beautiful mansions*
> *And are wearing the finest of clothes*
> *There are blue-blooded queens and princesses*
> *With charms made of diamonds and pearls...*
> *But the only real thoroughbred lady is The Rebel Girl...*

I wish she had been there, that old thoroughbred, to hear me sing for her. She would have deemed it just the right note, would have slapped her thigh in delight. In short, she would have loved it—and me for chancing it.

Step

A grandson of ours came home from school one day, about five years ago, at roughly 14 years old, and flung himself into a chair in his family's kitchen.

"In English class this afternoon we studied myths and fairy tales and I decided I *hate* stepmothers," he said to his own mother, with dark conviction.

She shot back at him, "What are you talking about? Don't you understand that Nana is my stepmother?"

He stopped, stupefied. "Nana is a *'stepmother'*?" he said, disbelief dripping from his lips. "But that can't be...I *love* Nana! In these stories, the stepmothers were always *awful*..."

That is one of my four much-loved grandchildren speaking—step grandchildren, to be precise. And that is my oldest stepdaughter answering, always disliking the word "stepmother" herself. I don't like the word either, but it draws a defining line around the territory I entered thirty years ago when I married Tom. He came into the marriage with two children, then teenagers; I came with none. Together we all built the stepfamily we are today—complete with the ambiguities that track us and every other stepfamily on the planet.

For me, a peculiarly difficult ambiguity stems from the sadness of not having children of my own. Despite Tom's and my strong desire for a child, it didn't happen. And by the time we reached our early forties, with previous marriages and divorces exacting their sorry tolls, adoption felt unwise.

One would think the sadness would fade over time—and of course it has. Thanks to the love that binds me to my husband, to my whole stepfamily, and to a deeply satisfying work life over many decades, everything has been woven into a richly-colored cloak that I prize intensely. A cloak I would never want to live without.

And yet. The emotional fallout from not having children of my own persists. Way down, it persists. Which means that while my stepfamily is an extraordinary blessing in my life, and a wellspring for my gratitude, they are *at the same time* unwitting reminders of loss, of lack, of dreams that didn't come true. They are, in other words—without seeking the role—the essence of a strenuous blessing. It could be put this way: although my stepdaughters and grandchildren have been powerful instruments of healing the heartache of childlessness in me, they also are paradoxically part of the reason the heartache still generates an echo of emptiness.

This counterpoint between full and empty, abundance and scarcity, has sounded in me for decades now like the tock of a metronome. Surely a similar counterpoint can be found in any life. None of us gets it all; all of us swing between sorrow and joy. But there is something so primal, so indelibly *absent* when wanted children are not born. Think of parents who yearn, without avail, for grandchildren. The wound created by this particular absence is ironic in its invisibility. Yet despite that invisibility, pain from the wound of childlessness can assert itself as steadily as a metronome's beat.

Having children—or not having them—obviously does not define a woman or define who she can be. But having children—or not—*does* profoundly alter a woman's sense of herself and the way the world views her. I'm aware that claims of "profound altering" may be quickly dismissed nowadays, but the childless woman in me still wants to shout *it's simply not accurate to do that.*

Consider a seemingly petty illustration: introductions in social situations. From the start, the girls have always winced when I named them as stepdaughters. It's plain they've resisted the "remove" of the term. And so have I; that remove inevitably gets thrust into any handshake. Yet omitting the "step" feels far worse to me because it's fraudulent to do so. If I'd already had children of my own when I joined up with my stepdaughters, I might well have sallied forth and introduced them as daughters. But, as it is, calling them "daughters" feels like a land grab for a country not mine. For thirty years my loins have reminded me over and over again that these are not my children, so I can't claim them—no matter how much I love them, no matter how central they are to the growth of my grateful heart.

Look at the same introduction through the lens of adoption. If I had an adopted daughter I would never introduce her as "my adopted daughter"—she'd be my daughter, plain and simple. Whatever remove may exist in the adoptive mother's experience, and surely there is one, she is nevertheless fully a mother in all but the birth sense, particularly if her child was adopted as an infant. She is essential to her child's life, and she knows it. Like any other mother, this essentialness, this fullness-of-mothering, forever alters an adoptive mother's reality and the language about her child.

That feeling of essentialness breaks down, though, for a stepmother without her own children. At least it does for me. Over the years I have so often felt like a non-essential "extra," someone who came along late and occupies a profoundly ambiguous position. This has nothing to do with how much I am loved by the rest of my stepfamily, or whether *they* see me as someone extra. I know they do not. It's simply a part of my own existential makeup, an aspect of the way that childlessness asserts itself in me.

All this took on added emotional complexity when the grandchildren started being born. From the first moments of their lives they were a phenomenal blessing to me; each of them only increased the depth of my gratitude. *And simultaneously,* a hollow in my heart rattled anew. That rattle had long preceded their arrival...it simply got louder. The following incidents will make the point.

Various arrows arc into the life of a stepmother without her own children. Such an arrow pierced me one morning, years ago, as I entered the vestibule of the church my husband and I were then serving in New York City. I was excited beyond measure: my younger stepdaughter had just given birth to a baby girl, the first grandchild, and I called out gleefully to an early gathering of parishioners milling near the door, "Hey! I'm a grandmother!" A woman in the group that I didn't know well but who knew enough about me to make this remark, said, "How can you possibly be a grandmother if you've never been a mother?"

In a related vein, nineteen years later, I was telling a story about this same granddaughter, having just visited her at college with Tom. The woman I was talking to, a long-time acquaintance, said, "Now, is that *Tom's* granddaughter you visited at college, or yours?" knowing perfectly well the answer before she asked. Granted that her question was obtuse, it still pressed me into saying, "She's my stepdaughter's child, so technically she's my step granddaughter." I added, with a distinct underscore, "After nineteen years, I think we can drop the 'step.'" She turned aside with the faint but unmistakable smile of a mother of three, knowing the step is never completely dropped. And she's right. Painfully right.

Addressing the discomfort of such moments is a

fraught business. If I draw attention to the oddness I experience in being a stepmother when I'm not also a mother, it makes me feel exposed, waspish, and ungrateful—as though I should give thanks for what I do have and shut up already about what I don't.

And yet arrows like these can sink deep. They strike into the singular isolation and loneliness a woman without her own children—stepmother or not—often feels. If she truly didn't want children, that's another matter. But if she did want them, and somehow never had them, she likely experiences a lot of vaguely articulated pity and awkward avoidance of the subject—as well as the occasional arrow—all of which increase her isolation. The only people who fully grasp this particular isolation are other childless women who wish they weren't. But we're a mostly silent group; we don't tend to talk much about the strangeness of the childless experience. After all, *something that is missing* doesn't normally arise as a subject for conversation since it exists only in the negative. And if it does get mentioned, it takes the form of a lament that finds no resolution simply by being voiced. Besides, a lament is often first cousin to a whine. As I said: it's fraught.

While it's true that the sadness of not having my own children has lessened a great deal, I still live in a world of grocery carts with chubby little legs crammed into back-facing seats. A world of tiny, stockinged feet, where the refrain of *one shoe off, one shoe on, diddle diddle dumpling, my son John*, can ring in my head without warning. A small face looks up from the perch in the cart; as I pass on to the avocados, the pot roast, the paper towels, an image of the face often remains. And long beyond the years when a child of my own might have become a reality, I still have to work at not being haunted by those shoeless feet. Such attempts usually fail: I am almost always caught wondering *what if, what if.* The wound may be invisible, but it is never totally quiet.

Plenty of people *with* children might respond to this by saying, *Let me tell you, cookie, having kids is not all it's cracked up to be.* Indeed, I gave a talk many years ago on the emotional vagaries of childlessness to a group of about fifteen women, most of whom had children. When one woman said, with a snorting laugh, "I'd be *delighted* to lend you mine for a few days," an embarrassed twitter traveled around the room. Each woman may have understood that trivializing a painful subject wasn't fair—but they could also identify with this bit of jaundice, knowing that children *themselves* turn out to be a strenuous blessing. Ask any one of those mothers, however, whether they would trade the bad days for no days at all and the answer would be unequivocal. As it would be—in a far darker key—for a woman with a child who has died.

Despite certain cultural assumptions, stepmothering doesn't "fix" things for the woman without children of her own. There's a straightforward reason. Just as a woman *with* children can't ever "un-know" the realness of them, so the woman *without* children can't ever "know" herself into a realness that doesn't exist for her. Once a woman has children, she automatically moves into a world that the childless woman, whether she's a stepmother or not, can't inhabit.

Childless stepmothers (the oxymoron is apt) occupy a region of "mothering" that's sort-of-real-but-isn't. And this not-quite-realness leads to various psychological snares. There's a specific hesitation, for example, around babies. I've talked to other stepmothers about this and have certainly felt it myself. It's a type of shyness, or lack of confidence, that comes from never having been charged with a baby's care. When my grandchildren were born, accordingly, I didn't spring to the fore to change their diapers. Someone might say *Come on, a diaper's a diaper.* But that isn't the point. The mother who becomes a grandmother (often after salivating over the prospect for a long time) is usually *fine* with diaper detail... taking a page from my siblings and friends, she can't wait! It has nothing to do with the diapers, of course; it has everything to do with relishing a brief return trip to her own young motherhood.

For a related gauge of the un-realness attached to stepmothering, notice what happens when older mothers encounter an infant, especially an infant born into their extended family. They tend to melt, shedding decades. Bending down to the baby, they revert in a flash to the most common word spoken by new mothers to their infant child for months, "Hi!" Whenever I've witnessed this, it has seemed like a moment of unguarded, solid gold re-membering—startling in its nakedness. To me, however, never having spent those months pouring myself into "Hi!" it sounds alien. I can find newborns just as compelling as any woman revisiting her own early motherhood. But it's for markedly different reasons, and it calls up a different language — largely interior.

Another oddity affecting the stepmother without her own children is the low level of curiosity that may come from one's original family in regard to stepchildren or grandchildren. Such lukewarm curiosity isn't mean-spirited or intentionally unkind. It's more an absence, a bell that doesn't get rung. The usual give-and-take that gathers around kids as they grow up, the normal interest in news or photographs or fortunes, simply doesn't occur much. It isn't that the stepchildren or grandchildren aren't "there," but their existence is mostly a blur on the edge of the family frame. Which makes a certain sense: those step-children or grandchildren aren't *in* the family frame in the same way that children born or adopted into a family are.

Here's the blunt point: what everyone knows, but rarely acknowledges, is that *there is no substitute* for having one's own child. There's no equivalent "state of being." It's as though mothers live on one side of a divide and non-mothers on the other. They may wave across the distance, but the country of each will ever and always be foreign territory to the other.

So there it is — or there is part of it. With that much said, though, and without calling the divide any less real, there's a parallel truth that is equally real: the divide can be emotionally redefined.

For the redefining to happen in my life, it wasn't simply that years needed to pass. It was more that a tumbler in my own heart had to turn over and unlock a reservoir of love. A host of incidents—some involving the girls, some the grandchildren, many connected to Tom—have been part of the unlocking. And, of course as the tumbler turned, the concepts of mother and stepmother got gradually transformed.

There was the time, for instance, when I suggested to my stepdaughters that we name ourselves differently: calling them my daughters-by-marriage, and me their mother-by-marriage. They loved the idea. As did their mother, Barbara, Tom's first wife, with whom Tom and I are friends. And so I morphed, into m-b-m. When I can reach past my own shyness, I now introduce them as my daughters-by-marriage. The term at least doesn't carry any whiff of fraudulence and I do know I am, beyond doubt, their mother-by-marriage. I can still hear the metronome's beat, but it's distant now.

Then there was the day Barbara said to me, with great insistence, "You're as much a mother to the girls as I am," urging that we take a photo of the two of us together and give it to the girls that year for a Mother's Day present. Tom later put this photo on the desk in his marriage counseling office, signaling to couples navigating the sharp rocks of divorce that real repair might someday be possible.

Or there was the morning, in a crowded first-grade classroom on Grandparents Visiting Day, when Tom and

Barbara and I all took our seats on some very short chairs. He and she were both bursting with pride; I was still not sure of my place in the scheme of bursting things. After a time, each child was asked to name one favorite thought or memory about a grandparent. As my granddaughter's turn came closer I was conscious of holding a slight breath. Then she lisped through her missing front teeth, grinned wide, and whispered, "My favorite is my Nana's coffee cake."

And then there are the multiple, loving cards that I've received from my daughters-by-marriage for decades now. Two of these are framed and hang on my home office wall. One, a Mother's Day card full of strong sentiment, is addressed to "the very best m-b-m ever!" The other, probably the sweetest birthday card I've ever received, shows a gold-edged painting of a woman with a teenaged girl curled up next to her and a text saying:

> *It's just like you to look out for me,*
> *Wish good things for me,*
> *And keep up with my life.*
> *It's just like you*
> *To love me*
> *As if I'd been yours from the very beginning.*

Way back when, I couldn't fully hear those words. Or let's say I couldn't bear to hear them. I should have paid closer attention to my tears, which never fail to appear when I re-read the cards. The tears come, of course, from a realm of deep loving and deeper home—a kind of cosmic Home Plate—a place much larger than I once realized, where I now know I belong to the children and grandchildren I have.

No, the step is never completely dropped. But for more than thirty years, my daughters-by-marriage have made it plain that the step is not the point. And the grandchildren, without conscious intent, have amplified that message to such a degree that I couldn't possibly miss it: *no matter how I arrived at this particular party, I've been their Nana from the beginning, and I'm not supposed to be anywhere else.*

If asked what that means, they would scratch out a list of regular, dependable, grandmotherly behavior: I'm the one who has kept track of their height measurements, every year, on the doorjamb of our kitchen. Who has baked their favorite picnic cake each summer of their lives—to whoops of delight. Who has given them books of poetry, mailed care packages to college dorms, showed up to cheer for them at athletic events. And still produces the same prized coffee cake every once in a blue moon.

Is the ambiguity gone? It's not meant to be. Since my grandchildren and my daughters-by-marriage will never be bone of my bone or flesh of my flesh, a complicated ambiguity is destined to remain resident in the chambers of my heart. It's like the splinter of sadness about not having my own children, probably lodged forever in those same chambers. In the end, though, neither of these shadows has a chance against the mid-day sunshine shed by my gratitude. As William Blake would put it, I've learned something about bearing the beams of love. And since I've felt those beams borne back to me, as steadily and reliably as the incoming tide, what more could one ask? The blessing remains strenuous, in its own strange way, but for this mother-by-marriage-turned-grandmother many years ago, it's a blessing that extends far beyond the telling.

Either We're Amused or We're Not

Skip this essay if you haven't turned sixty yet. Most of us need to pass into our sixties before mortality dawns on us for real and an unmistakable piece of news gets bugled in from stage left...time is short!

No matter what we might call that news, we're not usually disposed to call it amusing. The ancient psalm has it right:

> *Our days are like the grass;*
> *We flourish like a flower of the field;*
> *When the wind goes over it, it is gone,*
> *And its place shall know it no more.*

I love those lines. I also shiver in the shadow they cast. To ascribe "amusement" to them feels contradictory, even perverse. Yet it seems that the capacity to be amused is exactly what we need when the bugle blows and the fleetingness of life is borne in on us. The message is clear. If we want to live with gusto until the last song is sung, we have to find real delight in time's winged feet.

It's complicated, though. We tend to think of amusement as synonymous with funny. But when breasts droop, joints bulge, hips break, and memory clouds—let alone when serious illness strikes us or someone we love—we are a long way from funny.

I'm not using the word amusement that way. I mean amused *by life itself*, being quickened down deep by how extraordinary it is to be alive in the first place. To feel this amusement is to relish the unending ironies life brings. It's to have a sense of humor that refuses to be knocked off course by the inevitable punches life delivers. It means being able to gather all of life's beginnings and endings into one overflowing armful, throw our heads back in exuberant laughter and stride boldly forward—right through those disappearing flowers.

How difficult it is to pull this off, however. Or at least it is for me. I can reach for a high-spirited embrace of the process of aging and be uplifted when I manage it, but just as often all I can hear is my own muttering lament about bones and breakdown. The problem, of course, is this: if shortness of time is the trumpet's tune, death is the inescapable bass note. And when we hear that note, even if we have considerable trust in an afterlife—as I do—amusement may still be in short supply.

Which is the point. As we pass the thresholds of sixty, seventy, and beyond, real amusement can't exist *without*

inviting both life and death onto the dance floor simultaneously.
I thought I understood this at sixty. Clocking in now at
seventy-five, I see the reality painted in far more vibrant
colors. In my relationships with those I love—and whom I
quake at the thought of losing or of their losing me—life
and death not only stand next to each other, they are doing
an undeniably cozy waltz.

In childhood, the idea that life and death are *always* attached would have seemed absurd. But when we grow
older, we begin to get it. And we also get that all relationships gradually become, by definition, "short-term." As we
age, and then age further, loving inevitably develops a distinct shadow of poignancy around it—like the ring around
the moon when rain is coming. A certain kind of "funny"
may be in that shadow. But there's also an indissoluble
stripe of sadness. And the older we are, if we embrace being amused in the sense I'm suggesting, the undertone of
sadness never disappears.

Consider my love for an eleven-year-old grandniece of
Tom's and mine. She is so full of life that even a few
minutes in her company can short my aging cir-
cuits...deliciously.

On the day she arrived last summer with her parents
(and her equally loved, if quieter, older brother) from New
York City for the family's annual island vacation, Tom and
I drove to their house to greet them. She let out a shout
when she spied us and came cartwheeling across the lawn.
In a whirl of skinny legs and tousled hair she fetched up
beside our truck, beaming her megawatt smile. As Tom

opened the truck door and drew her in for a hug, she melted into his side like a sun-softened candy bar—and then straightened up fast and got ready to dash. There was, after all, a beach to inspect *now,* given the many months in Brooklyn without sand or rocks or tidal treasures.

She paused long enough to fling her arms briefly around my neck too and pepper me with ardent kisses, then peeled away to plunge down the dirt road toward the beach. I watched her leap into the gilded light of late afternoon. And as I remembered my own hurtling down the same road, at the same age, in the exact same light, I caught my breath once again at the awareness that for me all afternoons now are late ones.

Can we find the courage to be genuinely amused when we have to acknowledge how brief the time is we have left? Can we truly call it a blessing? It's a bind for me. I may talk a good game, but when right up against the reality of it my heart can seize. After all, I expect to be long gone before this grandniece gets a glimpse of her twenty-fifth birthday—which means, if all goes as usual, I will miss the lion's share of her life. Just as I will miss so much of my beloved grandchildren's lives. There is great rue in this thought.

A real measure of our children's contentment, however, depends on those of us who *are* old not making much noise about that rue or about what we'll miss. Our exit from the stage may be coming before long, but our job is still to be amused, in the widest sense of the word. And we can't give in to communicating our amusement, either, since it won't be comprehensible until those same children cross the threshold of old age themselves. That's one of the strangest features of growing older; the weirdness of it all eludes us until we get somewhere near the finish line. As does any answer to the primal struggle between holding on and letting go.

Of course we want to hold on tight. Every fiber in us wants to do that—never mind whether in our wisest moments we see the folly of it. Many years ago, looking to remind ourselves of this struggle, Tom and I asked an elderly artist friend on the island to hand-letter a piece of William Blake's poetry into a large square on our dining room wall. The letters have faded now, but the sentiment hasn't. It says:

> *He who binds to himself a joy*
> *Does the winged life destroy*
> *But he who kisses the joy as it flies*
> *Lives in eternity's sunrise.*

All our grandchildren have puzzled over the meaning of those words—unaware that they're *supposed* to be puzzled for now. Someday, though, many years after their grandfather and I have waved our last goodbyes and disappeared over the horizon, and they perhaps are enjoying the good fortune to be owners of the house, we hope that scrap of wisdom on the wall will have long since passed into their bloodstreams. I like to imagine the four of them and their various partners gathered at the dinner table over the remains of supper some summer night, laughing with one another over a last glass of wine—the sweet breezes drifting into the dining room from the screened-in porch, and the grandchildren only obliquely aware of those lines, only fleetingly conscious of how dearly we loved them while we had time.

Acknowledgments

Enormous thanks to:

My friend, fellow writer-in-arms, and peerless editor, Kate Kennedy. For all the encouragement she gave me, some of it while battling severe illness, I will always be grateful.

A group of ardent and helpfully critical readers: Nina Frost, Melinda Meisner, Kate Wilkinson, Sheila and Philip Jordan, Sharon and Bill Schambra, Joyce Wilson Sanford, and Jacqueline Simmons.

My dear daughters-by-marriage, Robin Cushman Philips and Tracy Callahan, for cheering me on in this project.

Ariette Scott, the most skillful computer wizard ever, and a boon companion in the endless task of creating a book.

And my husband, Tom, for his enduring support as a faithful reader of these essays, his editing skills, and his loving companionship in all things.

About the Author

Mary had an early and illustrious career as a waitress before graduating from the University of Southern Maine. She then worked as a community organizer, co-owned a vocational rehabilitation firm, and was co-founder and director of the first shelter for battered women in Maine. In the late 1980's she graduated from Yale Divinity School and was ordained an Episcopal priest. She and her husband, Tom, also a priest, worked for a decade in large urban parishes, and then maintained a counseling and spiritual direction practice in Portland, Maine, for almost two decades. They live on nearby Chebeague Island.

The Cushmans are the authors of *Riding the Passionate Edge*, published in 2014.

Made in the USA
Lexington, KY
07 February 2018